Space & Planets

TIME-LIFE
ALEXANDRIA, VIRGINIA

C O N T E N T S

1

The Solar System

In the vast and wondrous universe spin hundreds of billions of galaxies, each embracing billions of stars. One of these galaxies is our own Milky Way, and near one edge of it circles the star we call the Sun. From its place at the center of the Solar System *(right)*, the Sun provides us with warmth and light.

The Earth and eight other planets, some with moons, travel around the Sun. In order outward from the Sun, the planets are Mercury, Venus, Earth, Mars, Jupiter, Saturn, Uranus, Neptune, and Pluto. Countless asteroids and smaller chunks of matter revolve between Mars and Jupiter; several comets also orbit the Sun.

The picture at right shows how the Solar System looks, seen from just beyond Pluto; Neptune is at lower right. From that great distance, the Sun, even though it is by far the biggest object in the Solar System, looks small and faint. Comets have the oddest orbits in the Solar System, periodically swooping close to the Sun. Some comets also travel to the very edge of the Solar System, where they may gather bits of the original material from which the Solar System was formed.

This book will examine the Sun and the bodies visible in the night sky—the planets, moons, stars, the Milky Way, and other galaxies—and the missions into space that help scientists gain a better understanding of the universe. Chapter 1 looks at how the Solar System began.

The nine planets, asteroids, and a comet orbit the Sun in an artist's view of the Solar System.

How Did the Solar System Begin?

Although the Solar System is small when measured on the scale of the universe, it is vast from the perspective of the Earth. Light, which travels at 186,282 miles per second, takes 8.45 minutes to reach Earth from the Sun; it takes another five hours and 18 minutes to travel to Pluto. Over such huge distances, there is much we cannot see. But in painstaking observations through telescopes and space missions, astronomers have compiled information that helps explain the origin of the Solar System. Scientists believe that about five billion years ago, the Solar System formed in the stages shown below.

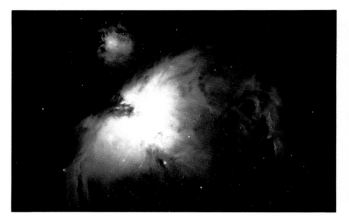

The Great Orion nebula is a birthplace for stars.

1 The original nebula. Some five billion years ago, a cloud of gas and dust, such as the nebula at right, broke away from a larger cloud in the Milky Way galaxy to form the Solar System. Gravitational pull in the center of the cloud drew matter inward and caused the cloud to contract and to spin.

2 A rotating disk. As the cloud revolved, the matter at the center became densely packed and extremely hot, forming the forerunner of the Sun. The gas and dust that surrounded the central bulge of the cloud flattened out and settled into an enormous disk.

3 Planetesimals form. While the center of the disk continued to heat, the outer rim cooled. Gas and dust condensed into particles, which began clumping together. The clumps became planetesimals—tiny planetlike bodies—of iron, nickel, rock, and ice. Perhaps a trillion planetesimals swarmed around the protosun.

Planets of rock or gas

The rock-type planets—Earth, Venus, Mercury, and Mars— are mostly solid matter and were formed by planetesimals that collided *(right)*. In the far- ther, colder reaches of the Solar System, the gas-type planets—namely Jupiter, Sat- urn, Uranus, and Neptune— were formed primarily of left- over gases *(far right)*. Pluto is a special case; it may be a rocky moon that escaped from Neptune's orbit.

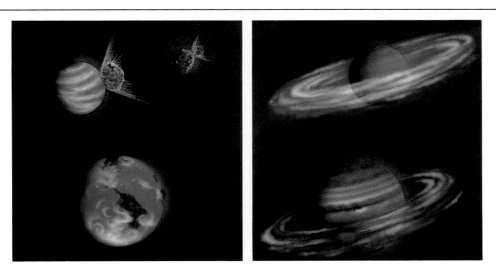

Formation of a rock-type planet   Formation of a gas-type planet

4 Planetesimals collide. When planetesimals smashed together, many of them shattered, but some would combine into one body. Larger planetesimals almost always absorbed smaller ones, and once a planetesimal began growing, each new collision made it larger.

5 Protoplanets form. Some of the largest plan- etesimals eventually gathered sufficient matter to become the nine planets. During this time, the protosun continued to gather matter to its core and became denser and hotter.

6 Moons form. Some left- over small planetesimals settled into orbits around plan- ets, becoming moons and rings. The protosun ignited its inner core and glowed. In the process, it stripped away lin- gering debris in a blast of solar wind that continues today.

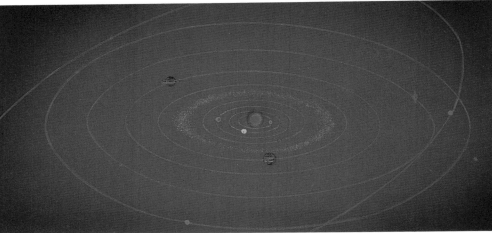

Why Is Mercury's Surface Cratered?

Mercury, the planet nearest the Sun, is small, hot, dry, and airless. Its gravitational field is too weak, compared with the Sun's mighty pull, to hold on to any gases, so it has no atmosphere. The Sun, looking twice as large as it seems from Earth, glares down on Mercury for a day that is as long as 88 Earth days. At noon, Mercury's surface temperature is 800° F., and in the middle of the equally long night, it dips to −300° F.—the largest temperature change on any planet in the Solar System. Mercury's barren, rocky surface preserves its earliest history, a tale of bombardment by meteors and comets crashing into the planet's surface and blasting craters of all sizes.

Mercury's pitted surface

A planet's scarred face. Photographed from space by the *Mariner 10* space probe in 1974, Mercury's surface is rough and pockmarked with craters.

Earth

Venus

An artist's conception of Mercury's bare, dry landscape—with Earth and Venus in the sky—shows how dust and rock shoot up from the explosive impacts of meteors. On Earth, dust from such a blast would form a large cloud. But on airless Mercury, dust and rock fall back to the ground, where the larger chunks of rock make craters in a circle around the central pit. These collisions cause vibrations but—because there is no air to carry them—no sound.

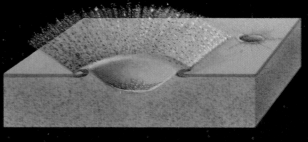

1 **A meteor's crash.** A meteor smashes into the surface of Mercury, throwing dust and rock up and out like splashing water. As there is no air to slow it down or blow it around, the debris quickly shoots high above the planet.

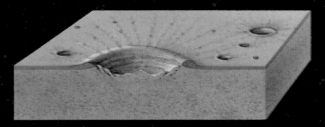

2 **A far-ranging descent.** Gravity slows the flight of the debris; dust and rock fall back to the planet. The biggest, fastest meteors make the largest craters. Their impact throws up the most rock and scatters it the farthest.

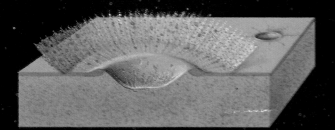

3 **Large and small craters.** The debris that is tossed up by the impact falls back onto the planet. Crashing to the surface in a ring around the first crater, the biggest chunks of the material blast out craters of their own.

4 **Rays from an impact.** The rock and dust that were thrown upward like a splash of water fall to the ground in rays. The fragments falling farther out from the center form patterns like spokes of a wheel. The largest, heaviest pieces land farthest from the center.

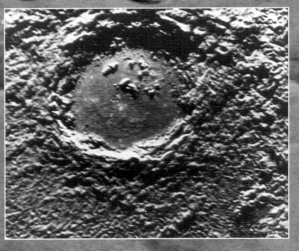

Crater ring. Most of Mercury's large craters, such as this one, are surrounded by many smaller craters that were caused by the same blast.

The second planet from the Sun, Venus, is Earth's nearest neighbor and almost matches Earth in size. Early astronomers imagined Venus as a lush paradise and called it Earth's twin. But recent space probes have given a very different picture. Within its thick, cloudy atmosphere, Venus is the hottest planet in the Solar System and is bathed in a drizzle of sulfuric acid, a corrosive mixture of sulfur, hydrogen, and oxygen. On the ground, the atmosphere is as heavy and dense as the water at the bottom of the ocean at a depth of 3,000 feet. But Venus has no seas, because the water long ago evaporated in the fierce heat. Scientists doubt that any life forms will be found on Venus.

A turbulent, violent world

Venus, as photographed by the U.S. Pioneer Venus-Orbiter spacecraft, is seen shrouded in dense clouds.

Nothing like paradise. With data gathered by space probes, scientists can piece together a picture of Venus's violent landscape *(above)*. Above a bare, lifeless terrain, shaped by volcanic eruptions, the sky is a deep orange color and thick clouds hide the Sun. Lightning flares, thunder roars, and sulfuric acid rains down. The Venusian atmosphere has almost none of the nitrogen and oxygen that sustain life on Earth. Instead, it is mostly carbon dioxide, the gas that humans and animals on Earth exhale when they breathe. At 900° F., this hot, dry atmosphere could melt lead or ignite paper, even at night. Each Venusian night lasts four Earth months because the planet turns so slowly in its stormy blanket of clouds.

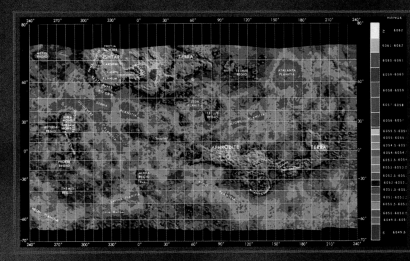

A radar map of Venus

Low hills and ridges appear in a radar photograph of Venus's surface *(left)*, detected under the planet's cloud cover by the United States' Pioneer Venus-Orbiter. On the other side of the planet are taller mountains that look like Earth's folded mountain ranges, such as the Himalayas. On Earth, these are formed during earthquakes, when plates, or sections, of the planet's crust shift, buckle, and fold. Scientists think Venus may experience the same kind of mountain-building, with violent Venusquakes.

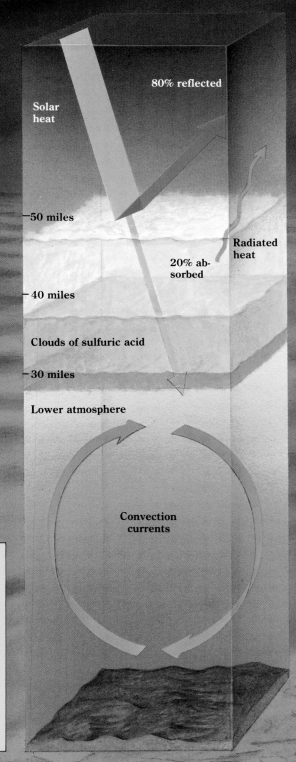

Solar heat

80% reflected

—50 miles

Radiated heat

20% absorbed

—40 miles

Clouds of sulfuric acid

—30 miles

Lower atmosphere

Convection currents

Venus's "greenhouse effect"

Three cloud layers in Venus's atmosphere *(right)* trap heat and keep the surface hot. Most of the heat from the Sun bounces off the outer cloud layer. The rest enters the atmosphere, warms the planet, and then cannot escape. The dense carbon-dioxide atmosphere thus keeps the surface hot even through the four-month-long night.

Inside Venus. The structure of Venus *(below)* is much like Earth's. The crust is thin and encloses a mantle of light elements, such as silicates, and a heavy metal core.

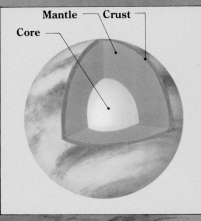

Mantle — Crust

Core

Could There Be Life on Mars?

Mars, the fourth planet from the Sun and Earth's other neighbor, glows with a reddish light in the night sky. Since ancient times, astronomers have called it the Red Planet and wondered whether Mars might support life. Though only half as big as Earth, Mars's day is 37.5 minutes longer than Earth's because Mars rotates more slowly. Its axis is tilted, like Earth's is, so Mars also has summer and winter seasons. But its atmosphere is thin and contains mostly carbon dioxide, and its surface is always well below freezing. Soil tests by two Viking missions in 1976 showed that iron oxide—rust—is the reason for the Red Planet's color. But the missions found no signs of life.

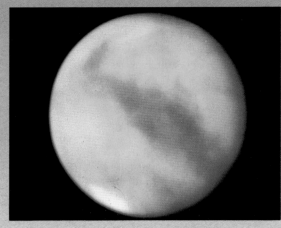

Polar icecaps. Seen as smudges of white, Mars's polar caps shrink and grow with the seasons. Astronomers think they are water and dry ice, that is, frozen carbon dioxide.

Mount Olympus

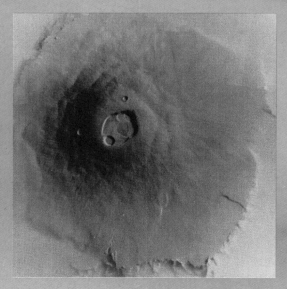

Mars's Mt. Olympus *(above and left)*, 15 miles high and 300 miles wide, is the biggest volcano in the Solar System. Discovered by *Mariner 9* in 1971, it is one of four huge Martian volcanoes, each about twice as wide and twice as high as Earth's volcanic island of Hawaii. All four Martian volcanoes seem to be extinct now. Their smooth, gently sloping sides were built up hundreds of millions of years ago by fast-flowing, hot lava.

Inside Mars. The structure of Mars is similar to Earth's. Volcanic eruptions took molten rock from the mantle to the crust.

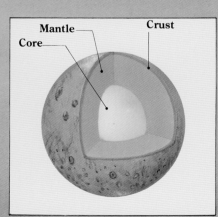

Mt. Everest *(white)* and **Mt. Olympus** *(gray)*

▶ **Closeups of Mars.** Red soil and rocks *(above)* under the orange Martian sky were photographed in 1976 by the *Viking 1* lander; one of the lander's jointed arms appears in the picture. A huge canyon, called Valles Mariner-is *(right)*, about 150 miles wide and 3,100 miles long, was photographed in 1971 by *Mariner 9*.

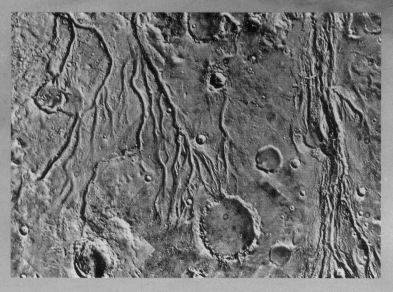

Dry riverbeds. Branching channels on the Martian surface resemble creek-and-river systems on Earth. Scientists believe water flowed freely when Mars was warmer.

What Is Jupiter's Great Red Spot?

Jupiter, the fifth planet, is the first of the gas-type planets. It is the giant of the Solar System, more than twice as massive as all the other planets combined. The lightest gases, hydrogen and helium, make up 99 percent of the planet; the remaining one percent consists mostly of a rocky core about the size of Earth. Revolving on its axis every 10 hours, this huge planet has the shortest day in the Solar System. Its ice-and-ammonia atmosphere contains one of Jupiter's mysteries: the Great Red Spot *(right)*. This prominent feature has baffled astronomers since it was first seen 300 years ago, but astronomers now understand that it is a huge and long-lived storm, though no one knows how it started.

Swirling gases. A Voyager photograph of the Great Red Spot shows a whirlpool of gases as big as two to three Earths.

Jupiter

Intricate winds form Jupiter's Red Spot

Direction of circulation

Low-pressure band

Gas down-draft

A storm in a turbulent sky

Jupiter's atmosphere is in constant motion. In the upper layers, gases of different colors reveal the wind patterns, in tinted stripes and spirals *(above)*. Lower in the atmosphere, alternating belts of rising or falling gases circulate in opposite directions about the planet and slip past each other without breaking up. The Great Red Spot *(center, right)* is a huge storm raging between two updrafts. It gets its color from a chemical that rises from the lower atmosphere and turns red in sunlight.

← **South**

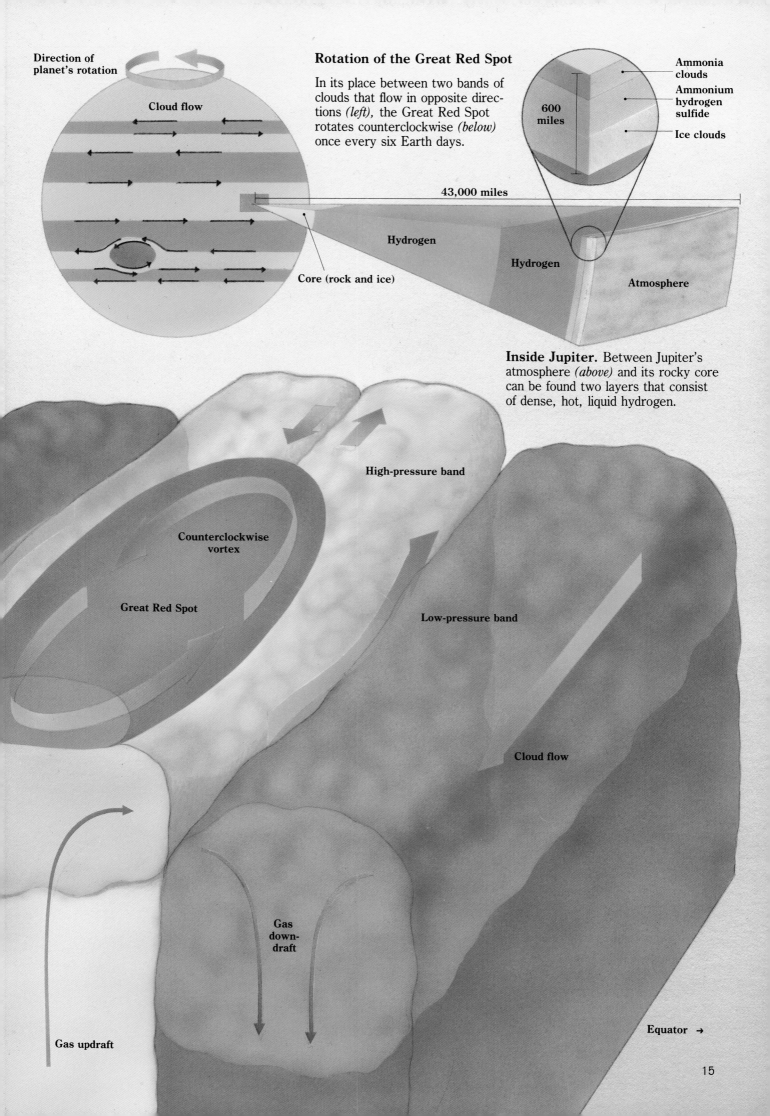

Direction of planet's rotation

Cloud flow

Rotation of the Great Red Spot

In its place between two bands of clouds that flow in opposite directions *(left)*, the Great Red Spot rotates counterclockwise *(below)* once every six Earth days.

Ammonia clouds

Ammonium hydrogen sulfide

Ice clouds

600 miles

43,000 miles

Hydrogen

Hydrogen

Core (rock and ice)

Atmosphere

Inside Jupiter. Between Jupiter's atmosphere *(above)* and its rocky core can be found two layers that consist of dense, hot, liquid hydrogen.

High-pressure band

Counterclockwise vortex

Great Red Spot

Low-pressure band

Cloud flow

Gas downdraft

Gas updraft

Equator →

Could Jupiter Have Become a Star?

Jupiter is the largest planet in the Solar System, but the Sun is 1,000 times larger. In fact, the two bodies are made of similar materials—mostly hydrogen—and only their difference in size has made them follow separate paths of development. Scientists calculate that just 100 times more matter would have made Jupiter's core hot enough to start a thermonuclear reaction, the explosive release of atomic energy that powers our sun and all other stars. As a star, Jupiter would have made the Solar System a different kind of place. But Jupiter was slightly too small and became a planet instead, in the stages that are shown here, starting with step 1, opposite.

Jupiter's stormy atmosphere, with its swirling currents and Great Red Spot, was photographed in 1979 by *Voyager 1* and *2.*

4 **Still cooling today,** giant Jupiter *(below)* dwarfs every other body in the Solar System, except the Sun, seen in the background at right. Jupiter's rings appear as a thin streak across the equator.

The young Jupiter aglow

Jupiter today

3 **With a core temperature** of perhaps 40,000° Kelvin, the young Jupiter glowed dark red. As the planet cooled, the glow ceased.

1 **About 4.6 billion** years ago, when the Solar System was forming, the core that became Jupiter began to grow from planetesimals of ice and rock. As the core *(far left)* became larger, it gathered more gas until a vast amount of gas surrounded it.

The developing Sun

The developing Jupiter

2 **Like the Sun,** Jupiter was a huge gas cloud that began to contract and heat up. But Jupiter's mass—the total of its matter—was much smaller than the Sun's. With less pressure on its core, Jupiter did not generate the heat needed to start nuclear fusion.

The young Sun

Young Jupiter

The Sun today

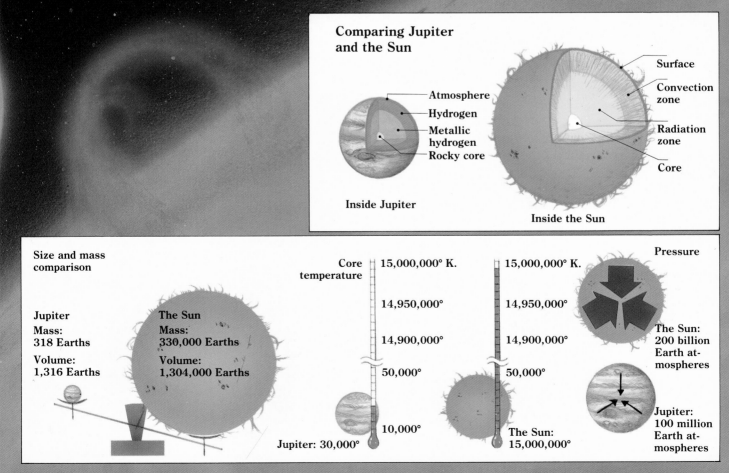

Comparing Jupiter and the Sun

Atmosphere
Hydrogen
Metallic hydrogen
Rocky core

Surface
Convection zone
Radiation zone
Core

Inside Jupiter

Inside the Sun

Size and mass comparison

Jupiter
Mass: 318 Earths
Volume: 1,316 Earths

The Sun
Mass: 330,000 Earths
Volume: 1,304,000 Earths

Core temperature

15,000,000° K.
14,950,000°
14,900,000°
50,000°
10,000°
Jupiter: 30,000°

15,000,000° K.
14,950,000°
14,900,000°
50,000°
The Sun: 15,000,000°

Pressure

The Sun: 200 billion Earth atmospheres

Jupiter: 100 million Earth atmospheres

17

Of Jupiter's 16 known moons, Io is one of the biggest—slightly smaller than Earth's moon. The Voyager missions' photographs of Io surprised scientists by showing 10 active volcanoes, some of them erupting. While Mars, Mercury, and the Moon have dead volcanoes, only Io, in all the Solar System, is more volcanically active than Earth. Volcanic ash and lava cover the scars of ancient meteorite collisions, and no part of the surface is even a million years old. The tidal stresses and strains that occur on Io in its orbit around Jupiter are believed to be the cause of the little moon's violent volcanoes.

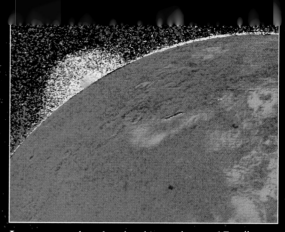

Io erupts. A volcanic plume shoots 17 miles into space in this picture of Io taken by the *Voyager 1* spacecraft.

Volcanic eruption

Gaseous sulfur ejected

Molten sulfur

Solidified sulfur and sulfur dioxide

Solidified sulfur and sulfur dioxide

Extremely hot, liquid sulfur

Crust (solid silicates)

Mantle (molten silicate)

Io's stressful orbit

Racing around Jupiter every 43 hours, with the same side always facing the planet, Io is wrenched with each trip by the tidal pull of Jupiter's immense gravity. Io's surface bulges toward Jupiter on its nearest approach and settles back down when farther away. The heaving of Io's rock-and-metal interior generates great heat, which powers its volcanoes.

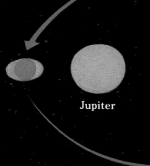

Jupiter

Io

The volcanic surface of Io

A volcanic jet of molten sulfur *(left)*, piped to the surface from a hot underground pool *(bottom left)*, showers over Io in a wide arc. Voyager's photographs of Io show a patchwork of orange and white splotches of erupted sulfur between small black patches of magma. Io's volcanoes do not build the high cone-shaped volcanic mountains seen on Earth. Instead, they are sunk deep into the surface, blasting hot liquids and gases up through cracks and crevices *(below)* with the speed of a bullet. Some eruptions reach as far as 190 miles high.

How Were the Rings of Saturn Formed?

Saturn, the sixth planet, is surrounded by a whirling, 250,000-mile-wide band of rings that are as thin as dust particles in some places. The rings are the most curious things about this giant planet, which is nine times larger than Earth. Scientists are not sure what caused the rings but think that they came into existence at the same time the planet was formed, some four billion years ago. When Saturn began to take shape from a spinning cloud of gas and dust, some of the dust particles were not drawn into this mass, perhaps because they were too light. They continued to circle around the planet, as they do today, like planetary debris.

Saturn's rings, photographed by *Voyager 2,* rotate individually around the planet.

1 **Too far from the Sun** to benefit from its warmth, the whirling dust particles that formed Saturn *(above)* were, for the most part, encased in ice. Bumping together while they circled through space, they gradually joined to form a larger mass, much in the way that snowflakes, under pressure, pack into a snowball.

2 **While Saturn was being born** *(right),* so too were its rings. Held close to the planet by its gravitational pull, some of the ice-coated dust continued to circle the planet and to arrange itself in concentric rings.

Planets with rings

For years, astronomers thought only Saturn had rings. Now at least three other planets—Jupiter, Uranus, and Neptune—have been found to have rings. Jupiter's rings *(far left)* are extremely thin. Uranus's narrow bands total 11 rings *(top near left).* Neptune *(bottom near left)* has four.

3 **In time,** the rings collected around Saturn's equator. The number of rings has never been counted, but judging from the slight variations in color that have been observed from band to band, there must be many thousands of them.

4 **The ice crystals and rock** from which Saturn's rings are formed *(below)* range in size from snowflakes to chunks that are as large as houses. Scientists believe that within each ring the crystals are constantly joining and separating. But the rings themselves scarcely seem to change their positions.

Is There Life on Saturn's Moon Titan?

Titan, the largest of Saturn's 18 moons, is the only moon in the Solar System that has an atmosphere. The scientists who planned the Voyager missions in 1978 eagerly hoped to learn whether that atmosphere was capable of supporting life. Some of them thought the air was like the atmosphere that existed on Earth when life began, four billion years ago. The space probe found a different mixture of gases and no liquid water; Titan's surface temperature of about − 289° F. keeps water frozen. But the atmosphere is rich in some chemicals that are part of what makes up life on Earth. Life may yet be discovered under the seas, where the temperature is higher.

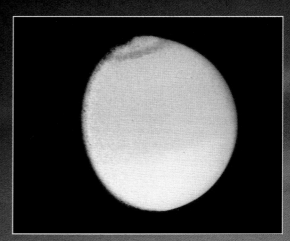

Hazy moon. Orange mist that is several hundred miles deep conceals Titan's surface in this photograph, which was taken by the *Voyager 1* mission. Scientists have scanned the surface with radar.

A cold, orange world. Under its dense nitrogen atmosphere, Titan probably has continents of rock, ice, and frozen carbon dioxide amid seas of sticky red-brown liquid ethane, which rains down from the methane clouds. The giant, ringed form of Saturn *(top right)* may sometimes show through the orange haze.

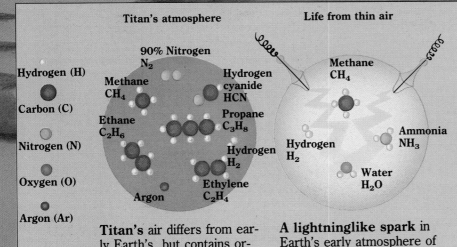

Titan's atmosphere

90% Nitrogen
N_2

Hydrogen (H)

Methane
CH_4

Carbon (C)

Hydrogen
cyanide
HCN

Ethane
C_2H_6

Propane
C_3H_8

Nitrogen (N)

Hydrogen
H_2

Oxygen (O)

Argon

Ethylene
C_2H_4

Argon (Ar)

Titan's air differs from early Earth's, but contains organic compounds, such as ethane, methane, propane, and ethylene.

Life from thin air

Methane
CH_4

Hydrogen
H_2

Ammonia
NH_3

Water
H_2O

A lightninglike spark in Earth's early atmosphere of methane, ammonia, and molecular hydrogen made amino acids, basic to life.

Could life develop on Titan?

A famous experiment *(left)* of 1953 showed that lightning flashing through the atmosphere as it existed on Earth four billion years ago joined certain molecules to form amino acids, the building blocks of living cells. Titan's atmosphere *(far left),* however, is not much like that of the early Earth, and is much colder; the Voyager mission detected no life there. But Titan does have the materials necessary for the formation of living cells, and scientists are hopeful that experiments performed on Titan will show how life began on Earth.

Why Is Uranus Turned on Its Side?

In our solar system, almost every planet's axis of rotation *(red lines, bottom right)* points, as Earth's does, roughly toward celestial north. The seventh planet, Uranus, is different. It makes its way through space spinning on its side, like a top that has run down. One possible explanation of this odd tilt is that Uranus was knocked sideways long ago, when another body smashed into it. The remains from this explosive crash may have formed Uranus's moons and rings later, in the steps shown on these pages. The Voyager mission, however, found no evidence to prove this theory or to suggest another.

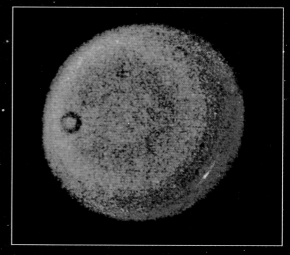

Computer image of Uranus. *Voyager 2* made this picture, which has been colored to show patterns in the Uranian atmosphere. Through the haze, one pole of the planet faces the Sun.

Axis of rotation

1 **A violent collision.** The developing planet Uranus was hit a long time ago by a planet-size body, which was as large as Earth. The intruder struck close to one of Uranus's poles, toppling the planet.

4 **Uranus today.** *Voyager 2* discovered two narrow bands in addition to the nine rings that can be seen from Earth. It also spotted 10 minor moons besides the five major ones that were previously known.

3 **Clouds become rings.** The clouds of water vapor, rock, and gas enveloping Uranus gradually settled into orbit around the planet's equator. This orbiting debris eventually became Uranus's rings and moons.

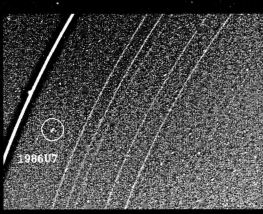

Rings and a moon. Uranus's rings and a previously unknown moon *(above)* were photographed for the first time ever by *Voyager 2.*

2 **Clouds of rubble.** The huge impact turned Uranus on its side, pulverized the intruder, and veiled the planet in clouds of water vapor and rocky debris.

● **Orderly axes**

Except for Pluto *(not shown),* the planets orbit the Sun in roughly the same plane, and the axes *(red lines)* on which they spin point less than 30° away from north. But Uranus *(green)* is on its side, turned almost 90°.

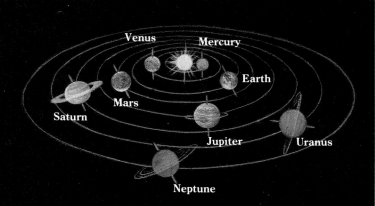

What Kind of World Is Neptune?

Voyager 2 (right) flew past Neptune *(far right)* on August 24, 1989. Its cameras made thousands of pictures of the eighth planet and its largest moon, Triton *(below)*, which is three-quarters as big as Earth's moon. Before ending its mission and disappearing into outer space, Voyager sent the pictures back to Earth, some 2.7 billion miles away. Voyager's data showed that Neptune is the windiest planet in the Solar System, with giant storms. The space probe also detected white clouds of methane, four thin rings, and six small moons besides Triton and Nereid, which were already known. But the real surprise was Triton. Voyager's images of Triton showed no impact craters but a rugged landscape. Astronomers named one region "cantaloupe terrain" because of its similarity to a melon's skin. Perhaps most amazing, Triton, with the coldest surface (−390° F.) in the Solar System, has active volcanoes.

Voyager 2

The surface of Triton

● **The coldest surface**

On Triton, Voyager found many ice-filled lakes with steep banks, almost certainly the craters of volcanoes. Mounds of frozen nitrogen and methane collect on the surface. The little moon's south pole is covered with a cap of nitrogen ice.

A serene blue from 220,500 miles away, Neptune is really the Solar System's stormiest planet, with winds of up to 1,500 miles per hour. The darker ovals are storms wider than Earth. The planet has four thin rings and eight moons.

Neptune

● The cold volcanoes of Triton

Unlike Earth's volcanoes, which expel hot, molten rock, Triton's cold volcanoes seem to spew liquid nitrogen. Nitrogen is the most plentiful gas in Earth's atmosphere, but in Triton's intense cold temperatures, its form is liquid. Scientists are of the belief that some nitrogen rises from underground as a vapor *(above)*, then falls back as nitrogen snow.

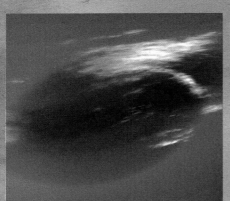

▲ **The Great Dark Spot.** In Neptune's atmosphere, dark oval patches like this are huge storms.

▲ **Complete rings.** Voyager saw four rings around Neptune that are all but invisible from Earth.

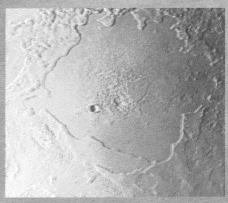

▲ **Mysterious crater on Triton.** This may be the vent of a volcano that once spewed liquid nitrogen.

How do astronomers know so much about planets that no one has ever visited? They observe planetary motion, from Earth or from spacecraft like Voyager, then apply physical and mathematical principles to their data. From a planet's volume—how much space it occupies—and its mass—how much matter it contains—astronomers are able to compute its density. Density is a measure of how tightly packed a body's matter is. Water is the standard of density and is given a value of 1; rock is more dense and air is less dense. Earth's density is 5.52. All planets are either dense, rock-type planets, such as Earth, or much less dense, gas-type ones, such as Jupiter. As shown in the illustrations below, the gas-type planets are hundreds of times larger than the Earth in volume but are made of very loosely packed material.

Stargazer. Set on Mauna Kea, Hawaii, above much of Earth's interfering atmosphere, this giant telescope is used to study the composition of planets and stars through a method known as infrared spectroscopy.

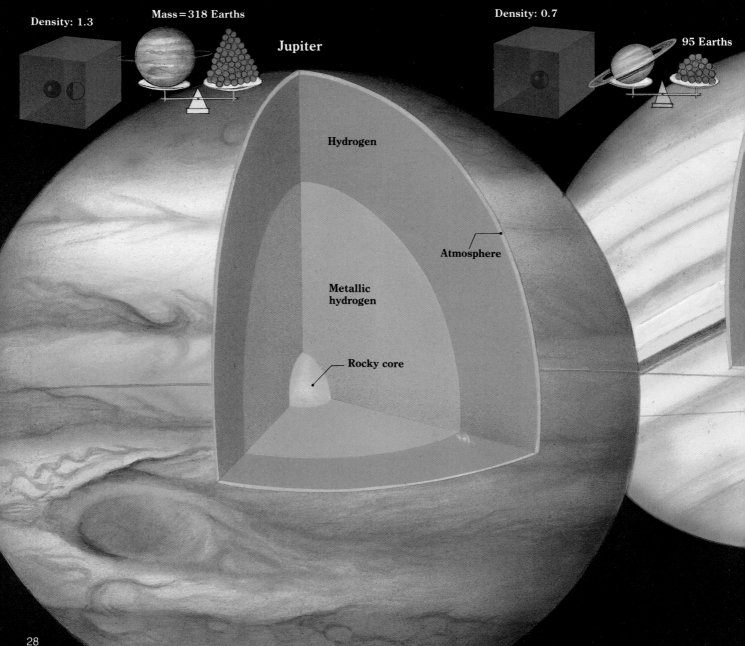

Density: 1.3

Mass = 318 Earths

Jupiter

Density: 0.7

95 Earths

Hydrogen

Atmosphere

Metallic hydrogen

Rocky core

● Infrared spectroscopy

By analyzing the radiation from a star or a planet, astronomers can find out what the body is made of. They use a spectrograph, which spreads light into its full spectrum of wavelengths *(top right)*. The dark lines, called absorption lines, form when an element absorbs light between the viewer and the source. Each element has its signature in a sequence of lines. Astronomers identify these "fingerprints" by comparing them with spectra produced in a laboratory. The spectrum of Jupiter has many absorption lines, indicating the presence of a variety of elements and molecules, including hydrogen and ammonia. The graph shows the same data with depressions—where light is absorbed—for hydrogen and ammonia.

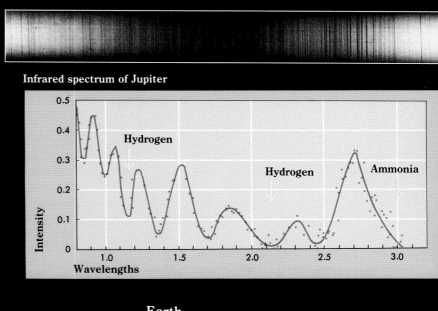

Infrared spectrum of Jupiter

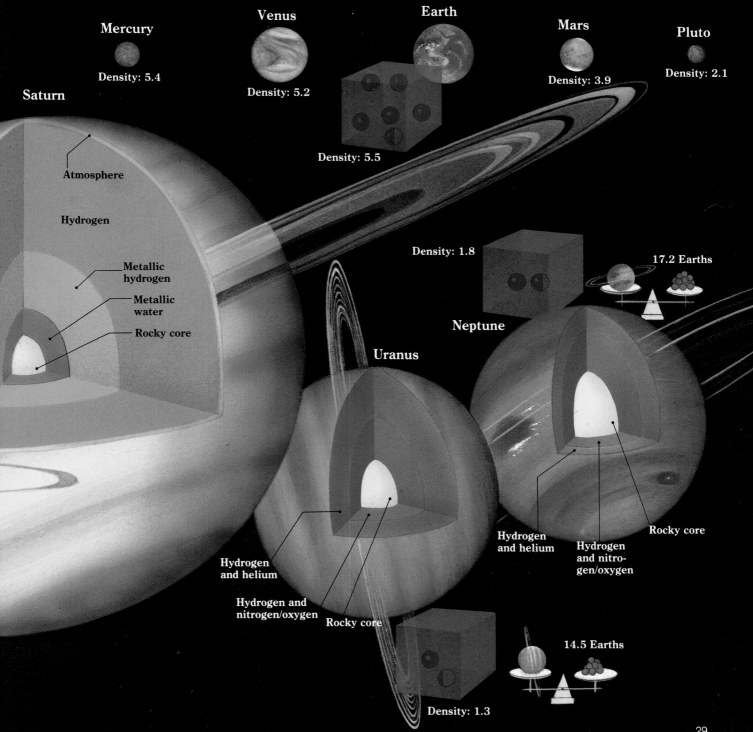

Mercury
Density: 5.4

Venus
Density: 5.2

Earth
Density: 5.5

Mars
Density: 3.9

Pluto
Density: 2.1

Saturn
Atmosphere
Hydrogen
Metallic hydrogen
Metallic water
Rocky core

Density: 1.8

17.2 Earths

Neptune

Uranus

Hydrogen and helium

Hydrogen and nitrogen/oxygen

Rocky core

Hydrogen and helium

Hydrogen and nitrogen/oxygen

Rocky core

14.5 Earths

Density: 1.3

How Were the Asteroids Formed?

Between Mars and Jupiter lies the asteroid belt—a region in which uncounted thousands of rocky planetary bits orbit the Sun. By 1990, scientists had logged and calculated orbits for more than 3,300 of the asteroids. There may be hundreds of thousands more, including those that are too small to be visible from Earth. The astronomers who discovered the asteroid belt thought it had been created when a planet that was in an orbit between Mars and Jupiter broke apart in Jupiter's powerful gravitational field, leaving fragments to continue moving in the same orbit. Today, however, the scientists believe that Jupiter's mighty gravity prevented the asteroids from ever merging into a planet in the first place. Because they may be leftover raw materials from one of the early stages of planet formation, the asteroids are capable of revealing much about the history of the Solar System.

Phobos, a former asteroid. This tiny Martian moon may be an asteroid that was pulled into orbit around Mars. No clear pictures of asteroids have yet been made.

Why the asteroids stayed small

The asteroids were forced into high speeds by Jupiter's gravity. When they collided, they rarely merged *(top right)*. More often, they would crater *(top left)*, chip *(bottom right)*, or demolish *(bottom left)* each other.

The orbits of asteroids

Most of the asteroids orbit the Sun in the asteroid belt, a zone *(below)* that is nearly a million miles wide and lies between the paths of Mars and Jupiter. Some, however, travel in greatly elongated—eccentric—orbits *(right)* that bring them near the Sun, and sometimes near the Earth. Apollo travels with a pack of other asteroids *(page 34)* that regularly pass close to Earth. In 1972, a small asteroid even bounced off the Earth's atmosphere, appearing as a bright streak across the sky. The likelihood of a large asteroid striking Earth's surface is remote. It might occur once every 250,000 years.

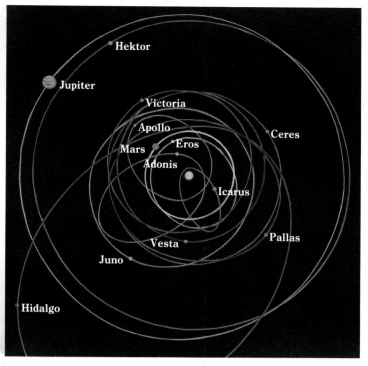

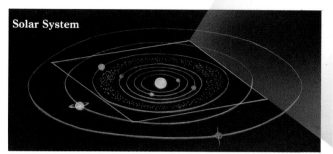

Solar System

Some major asteroids

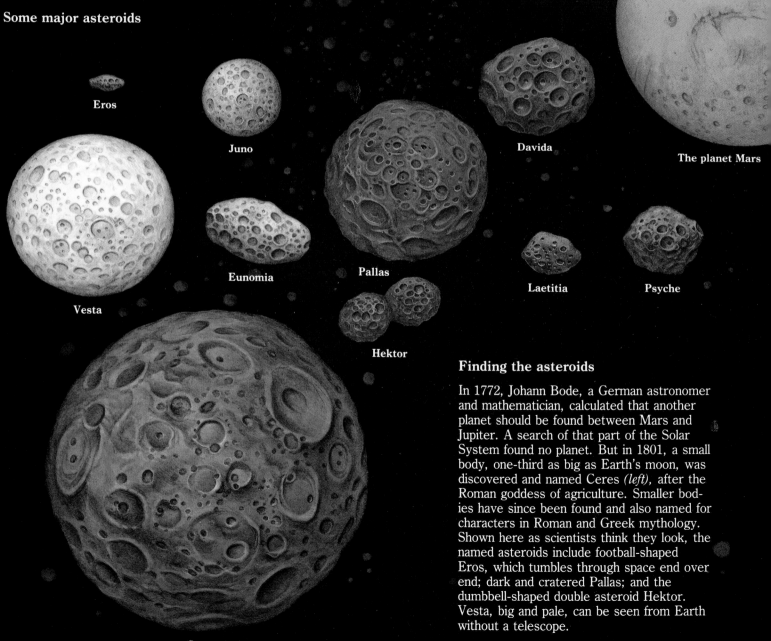

Eros

Juno

Davida

The planet Mars

Eunomia

Pallas

Laetitia

Psyche

Vesta

Hektor

Finding the asteroids

In 1772, Johann Bode, a German astronomer and mathematician, calculated that another planet should be found between Mars and Jupiter. A search of that part of the Solar System found no planet. But in 1801, a small body, one-third as big as Earth's moon, was discovered and named Ceres *(left)*, after the Roman goddess of agriculture. Smaller bodies have since been found and also named for characters in Roman and Greek mythology. Shown here as scientists think they look, the named asteroids include football-shaped Eros, which tumbles through space end over end; dark and cratered Pallas; and the dumbbell-shaped double asteroid Hektor. Vesta, big and pale, can be seen from Earth without a telescope.

Ceres

What Is a Comet?

Crossing the night sky, trailing a long, glowing tail, a comet is a spectacular sight. Comets are part of the Solar System and orbit the Sun. But compared to planets, they are tiny and their orbits *(right)* are tilted and elongated. Until they approach the Sun, comets are dark chunks of rock and ice. Then the Sun's radiation vaporizes some of the material. Dust and gases spurt from the nucleus, or core, *(bottom right)* to form the comet's head, or coma, and tail; these catch the Sun's light and seem on fire. Though a comet's nucleus is only a few miles wide, its coma can span several hundred thousand miles and its tail 6 million miles. Charged particles from the Sun—called solar wind—push against a comet's tail, making it stream away from the Sun, even when the comet is retreating from the Sun. Halley's comet is the most famous of comets.

The closest look yet at a comet

When Halley's comet came back around the Sun in 1986, after its usual absence of 76 years, five space missions were sent to meet it. They found a peanut-shaped nucleus *(right),* about 10 miles by five, surrounded by a turbulent, dusty coma that was several thousand miles across within a dim corona of gas several million miles wide. The nucleus—which probably consisted of boulders held together by ice—had craters and hills, rotated about its axis once in about two days, and had a black, tarlike substance all over it.

Orbit of the
Encke comet

Close, closer. About 300 million miles away, Halley's comet streaks across the night sky *(above)* in a 1986 photograph taken from Earth. A closeup view *(left)* of its oblong nucleus, photographed by a spacecraft 375 miles away, shows a jet of vaporized gas shooting from the bright sunward side.

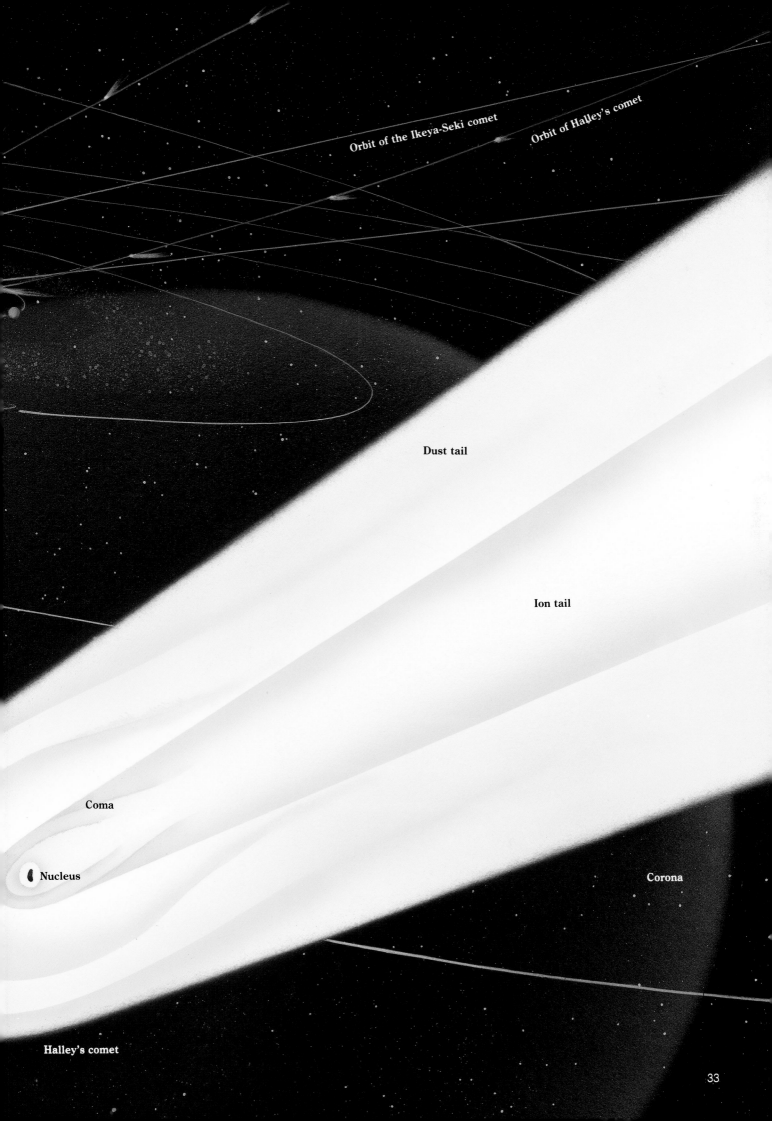

Orbit of the Ikeya-Seki comet

Orbit of Halley's comet

Dust tail

Ion tail

Coma

Corona

Nucleus

Halley's comet

What Are Shooting Stars?

On a clear night, you might see about five shooting stars in the space of an hour. These fast-moving points of light are not stars, however, but bits of rock and metal, which range in size from specks of dust to chunks that are as big as a house. When these bodies are out in space, the name for them is meteoroids. Pulled by Earth's gravity, meteoroids enter Earth's atmosphere at speeds of 10 to 44 miles per second. Heated to white-hot by friction, they draw lines of light across the sky and are called shooting stars, or meteors. Most meteors are entirely burned up as they travel through the atmosphere, but some survive to crash into Earth's surface, where they are then called meteorites. The Earth is struck by meteors every day and even gains 10 tons a day this way. The largest meteorite known is the 60-ton Hoba meteorite, which fell to Earth in Namibia, in southern Africa.

An iron meteorite. This 385-pound meteorite, found in Japan in 1885, is of meteoric iron, an iron-nickel compound. It looks polished by its passage through Earth's atmosphere. Some meteorites are rock, some are meteoric iron, and some are both.

The Apollo asteroids

Meteor shower

A glowing meteor

● **Meteorites across Earth's path**

Interplanetary travelers of many sizes cross Earth's orbit. Coming mainly from the asteroid belt, meteors rain down on Earth at random; they are called sporadic meteoroids.

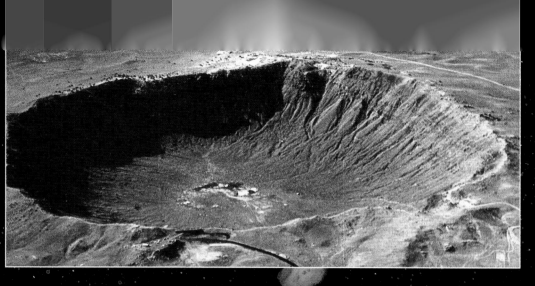

A meteorite crater. Eight-tenths of a mile wide, this crater in the Arizona desert is known as the Barringer Crater. It was made more than 20,000 years ago, when a meteor about the size of a railroad car landed here, blasting 400 million tons of rock into the air.

Comet

Gas and dust from a comet

● **Asteroid orbits**

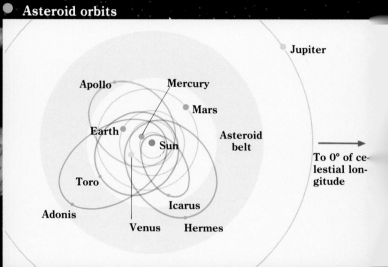

Jupiter

Apollo Mercury

Mars

Earth

Sun

Asteroid belt

To 0° of celestial longitude

Toro

Icarus

Adonis

Venus Hermes

Close calls. Some asteroids from groups that orbit near Earth may have become meteorites that blasted craters on Earth.

● **Meteor showers**

Meteors usually arc through the sky singly and come from all directions. But in a meteor shower, a hundred meteors may fall in an hour, all coming in one direction. Astronomers think most meteor showers result from dust that was left in space by passing comets. When they meet the Earth's atmosphere, these dust particles burn up. Annual meteor showers are named for the constellations in which they seem to occur—Leonids in Leo, Orionids in Orion, Perseids in Perseus, and so on.

2
The Sun

Sunlight pours forth from the Sun's interior at a speed of 186,000 miles per second—about 670 million miles per hour—giving life to all of Earth's organisms.

A swirling cloud of gas near one edge of the Milky Way galaxy gave birth to the Sun about 4.6 billion years ago. Today, it is a medium-size star, composed largely of hydrogen and helium. At the Sun's core, which burns at 15 million° Kelvin, pressure converts hydrogen nuclei into helium, producing vast amounts of energy in a process called nuclear fusion. The energy rises and, coupled with the Sun's rotation and magnetic forces, keeps the surface churning and sizzling. In some areas, magnetic forces cool the gas, forming dark sunspots visible from Earth. The number of sunspots grows and shrinks in 11-year cycles.

Occasionally, pent-up solar energy bursts from the chromosphere, shooting jets of gas, or flares, thousands of miles into space. A stream of particles, called solar wind, escapes through open magnetic field lines from the corona into space, its power only noticeable on Earth during maximum solar activity, when magnetic storms disturb compasses and power and communications systems, and light the skies with auroras.

In about five billion years, the Sun will begin a slow death, first expanding up to 100 times its present size, then collapsing until it is 100 times smaller than it is today. Its nuclear fires burned out, the Sun will become a cold, black cinder.

A solar flare arches 8,000 miles above the Sun's surface. The entire Earth could fit under the arch.

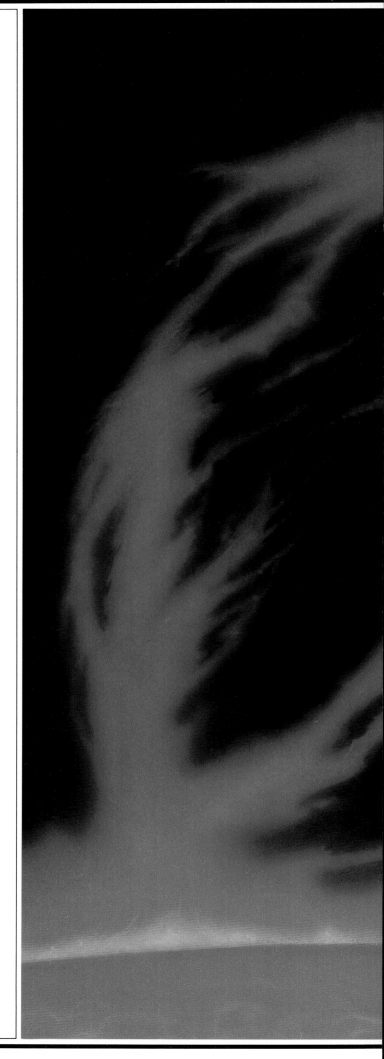

Where Did the Sun Come From?

Like all stars, the Sun formed from a contracting cloud of gas and dust. Gas particles on the outer edge of the cloud, or nebula, began to fall to the center, and their combined gravity pulled more atoms inside. For about 10 million years, the gas cloud grew denser and hotter. Then an important change took place at its core. Because of the gravitational pull, the increased pressure forced the atomic nuclei to fuse in a process called nuclear fusion reaction, releasing tremendous amounts of energy. With its nuclear fires lit, the Sun had become a star.

1 **A contracting gas cloud**

About five billion years ago, a concentration of luminous gas and dust, a nebula, began to clump and contract. Like pizza dough thrown spinning into the air, this nebula flattened into a disk, bulging at the center.

2 **Gravity's pull**

As the nebula continued to spin, gravity pulled matter to the center. More and more gas atoms fell inward toward the core, boosting density and temperature. As a result, the hot inner core began to glow.

The Sun today—4.6 billion years old
Brightness: Twice as bright as the
average star in the galaxy
Diameter: 864,950 miles
Core temperature: 15 million° K.

5 The Sun today

Now 4.6 billion years old, the Sun
has burned about half of the hydrogen that is in its core but will continue its nuclear burning for a period lasting another five billion years.

4 A star is born

After collapsing for 10
million years, the new-
born Sun stabilized at
slightly larger than its
present size. The core
temperature had reached
10 million° Kelvin and
nuclear reactions began.

100 million years old
Brightness: Two-thirds as
bright as the Sun today
Diameter: 800,000 miles
Core temperature:
15 million° K.

1 million years old
Brightness: Twice that
of the Sun today
Diameter: 4 million miles
Core temperature:
4 million° K.

3 Almost a star

Contracting still further, the bright
core collapsed to a size that was
about 50 times larger than the Sun
is today. Atoms continued falling
into the core, where intense gravity began smashing them together.

100,000 years old
Brightness: 10 times that
of the Sun today
Diameter: 7 million miles
Core temperature:
800,000° K.

10,000 years old
Brightness: 90 times that
of the Sun today
Diameter: 18 million miles
Core temperature:
75,000° K.

1,000 years old
Brightness: 500 times that
of the Sun today
Diameter: 45 million miles
Core temperature:
15,000° K.

What Is the Sun Made Of?

Like a flaming onion 110 times bigger than Earth, the Sun consists of several layers around a core. Hydrogen gas makes up about three-quarters of the Sun and helium nearly one-quarter, with a tiny fraction of other elements. The total amount of material in the Sun, its mass, is small compared with its volume, the amount of space it occupies, which means the Sun's overall density is low. But at the core, its matter is so densely packed that a piece the size of a walnut would outweigh a watermelon. Energy from the core's nuclear fire radiates through a middle layer. Farther out, a convection zone transfers heat from the inner region to the surface, or photosphere, that part of the Sun we can see. Above the photosphere lie two layers of atmosphere, the chromosphere and the corona, which are not normally visible from Earth.

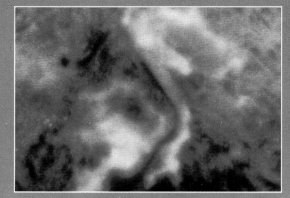

▲ **A bright flare** violently releases the energy of the Sun in a spurt of gaseous matter, also known as plasma.

■ **The structure of the Sun**

Core: Under 200 billion times the pressure of Earth's surface, hydrogen is fused into helium.

Radiation zone: Energy from the core rebounds here for centuries before surfacing.

Convection zone: Energy from the radiation zone enters a cooler layer of gas in the convection zone. The hot gas rises toward the surface, then cools and falls back again in turbulent convection currents.

Photosphere: Most of the sunlight we see beams toward Earth from the Sun's pebbly surface, or photosphere.

Chromosphere: This frothy lower layer of the solar atmosphere displays fountains of flaming gas such as filaments and flares.

Neutrinos: The fusion of hydrogen into helium in the core produces these chargeless, nearly massless subatomic particles.

Gamma rays: Fusion produces gamma rays, the most energetic form of electromagnetic radiation.

Corona: The Sun's outer atmosphere, known as the corona, fades gradually into space.

40

▶ **Different views of the Sun:**
1. The corona, during a total eclipse.
2. A hole in the corona in an x-ray photograph.
3. Bright hot spot and dark cold spot of the chromosphere in ultraviolet light.
4. Sunspots on the photosphere.

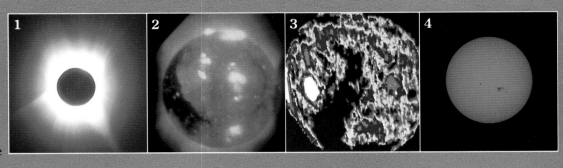

The Sun's outer shell: The photosphere, glowing at 6,000° Kelvin, hides all other layers of the Sun. The chromosphere blazes at 10,000° Kelvin, but appears a thousand times dimmer than the photosphere. The corona surrounds the Sun at temperatures as high as 2 million° Kelvin, but the gas particles are widely dispersed so that the overall heat of the corona is markedly lower. Its visible light, about as bright as the Moon, can only be seen when the Moon blocks the photosphere during a solar eclipse.

15 million° K.

6.5 million° K.

2 million° K.

6,000° K.

Convection zone
60,000 miles

Core
60,000 miles

Radiation zone
300,000 miles

Photosphere 300 miles

Chromosphere 1,500 miles

Plages: Glowing plages—from the French word for beaches—hover in the chromosphere above magnetically active regions like sunspots.

Prominences: Bright loops or sheets of gas, called prominences, may hover for days in the corona or explode and disappear in minutes.

Flares: The most spectacular effects of intense magnetic activity, flares can spew gas more than 150,000 miles into space.

Faculae: Bright patches, called faculae, loom in the upper photosphere, forming shortly before the appearance of sunspots.

Sunspots: Sunspots appear as dark specks on the surface of the photosphere. They are the only solar activity observable with the naked eye.

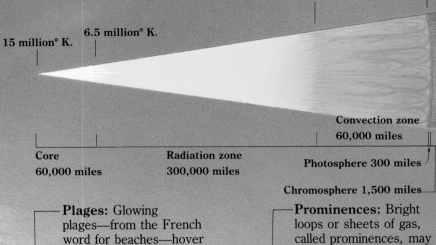

Spicules: Chromospheric gas columns, called spicules, shoot as far as 10,000 miles into the corona at 15 miles per second.

Granules: Flows of hot and cool gas roil the photosphere into 600-mile-wide granules and 18,000-mile supergranules.

41

What Causes Sunspots?

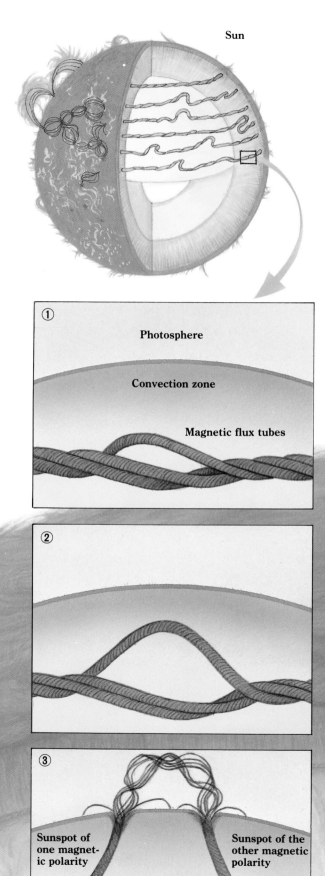

Sun

Photosphere

Convection zone

Magnetic flux tubes

① ② ③

Sunspot of one magnetic polarity

Sunspot of the other magnetic polarity

Magnetic flux tubes

Sunspots look dark on the Sun's surface because the cool gas they contain is dimmer than their hot surroundings. Even so, a sunspot is so hot it shines 10 times as brightly as the Moon. Sunspots form in an intricate process: The Sun rotates on north and south magnetic poles, but because the Sun consists of gas, its equator rotates faster than its poles. As a result, magnetic field lines—normally running from pole to pole—are dragged around the equator and become twisted. Convection currents add to the turmoil, bundling and braiding the field lines until they kink and pop through the photosphere, arching into the corona like a giant horseshoe magnet. The distorted field lines slow the convection currents, which in turn cool the gas and create sunspots. Often, one sunspot forms where a loop leaves and another appears where it reenters.

Magnetic twists and loops. 1. The gaseous Sun rotates faster at the equator than at the poles, causing magnetic field lines to twist into ropelike flux tubes parallel to the equator. 2. Hot gas rising through the convection zone lifts the magnetic flux tubes so that they float to the surface in loops. 3. As a loop breaks through the photosphere, each leg pins gas in place, slowing convection and allowing the surface to cool.

Convection zone

Magnetic flux tubes

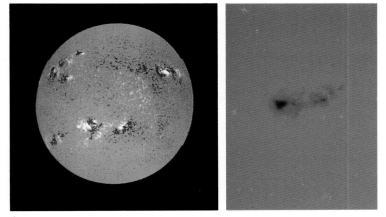

A magnetogram *(above left)* shows strong magnetic fields—dark and light areas—that surround sunspots. Sunspots *(above right)* dot the photosphere, as seen in visible light.

The 11-year sunspot cycle

Astronomers have observed sunspots for more than 2,500 years. For several hundred years, they have recorded sunspot cycles of roughly 11 years. As shown below, the average number of sunspots varies; periods of unusually large numbers are called sunspot maximum, years with unusually low numbers, sunspot minimum.

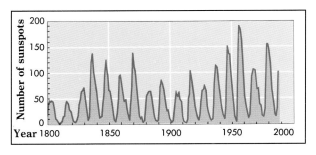

Magnetic field lines

Prominence

Sunspot

Sunspot

Chromosphere

Photosphere

What Makes the Sun Shine?

The core of the Sun burns with a ferocity beyond earthly fire. Its heat and light come from nuclear fusion, a process that fuses lighter atomic nuclei into heavier ones. Fusion reactions also convert mass into energy according to Albert Einstein's famous equation $E=mc^2$ (energy equals mass times the speed of light squared). In the Sun's core, hydrogen fuses into helium, converting some 4 million to 5 million tons of mass each second into energy.

1 Two hydrogen nuclei—each a single proton—collide.

One proton changes into a neutron. A positron and a neutrino escape.

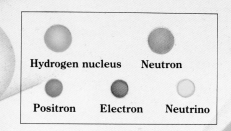

Hydrogen nucleus Neutron

Positron Electron Neutrino

Energy produced

2 A deuteron nucleus, with one proton and one neutron, approaches a hydrogen nucleus, or proton.

3 A deuteron nucleus and a proton collide, which results in the formation of light helium.

4 Two light helium nuclei are on a collision course.

■ Nuclear fusion

An atom's core, or nucleus, contains one or more protons and may contain one or more neutrons. Electrons orbit the nucleus. In the Sun's interior, intense pressure and heat strip off electrons, leaving a cauldron of naked nuclei. The pressure and heat also smash protons together, forging helium nuclei from hydrogen nuclei in three steps. First, two hydrogen nuclei, consisting of single protons, fuse to form one deuteron nucleus, releasing a positron and a neutrino. Next, the deuteron, or heavy hydrogen nucleus, and another proton join to become light helium, giving off energy in the form of a gamma ray. Finally, two light helium nuclei fuse, releasing two of the protons. The resulting helium nucleus, consisting of two protons and two neutrons, contains a little less mass than the protons had originally—mass that was converted into energy.

7 Expelled protons become raw material for other later collisions.

Energy produced

▲ **The Sahara,** just north of the equator, with little cloud cover, receives more solar radiation than any other place on Earth.

▲ **Nuclear fusion on Earth** is still in the experimental stage, as in the fusion reactor at Princeton University in New Jersey *(above)*. Unlike nuclear power plants that generate electricity through fission of rare metals like uranium, a fusion plant can use a common gas like hydrogen.

5 Two protons and two neutrons fuse. The excess protons break away.

6 An atom of ordinary helium, containing two protons and two neutrons, forms.

How Long Will the Sun Shine?

4.6 billion years ago. The core reaches 10 million° Kelvin, triggering hydrogen fusion.

Hydrogen

Today's Sun. Stable fusion reaction will heat the core for another five billion years.

Hydrogen

Helium

A star of average mass, the Sun has a life span that was fixed at birth. The more mass, the shorter a star's life. As stellar mass increases, so does gravity, and higher gravity in a star's core boosts heat. The most massive stars burn the hottest, living flashy, short lives. Small, low-mass stars fuse hydrogen slowly and live tremendously long lives. The Sun falls between these extremes.

5 billion years from now. The Sun has fused much of the hydrogen into helium. To maintain its temperature, internal fires burn more fuel, and the Sun expands into a bigger, brighter star.

Hydrogen

Helium

Hydrogen

Helium

Solar prominences. Magnetic disturbances can spew gas thousands of miles out into space. As the gas in a prominence curves upward and falls back to the surface, it follows the path of arched magnetic field lines.

Now halfway through its life, the Sun will continue to shine almost unchanged for another five billion years. Our star formed when a huge cloud of gas—about 75 percent hydrogen and 25 percent helium—collapsed into a hot, dense ball. Ten million years later, hydrogen fusion began in its center. The gas cloud had become a star. Today, after 4.6 billion years of shining steadily, roughly half of the hydrogen in the core has been converted to helium. This has barely changed the Sun's overall makeup. But when all the hydrogen is gone, the Sun will enter old age, beginning with some rapid changes. As the core begins to collapse, the Sun will briefly expand to 100 times its present size, the so-called red giant stage, engulfing Mercury and Venus and destroying life on Earth. Then helium in the core will fuse explosively, collapsing the Sun into a burned-out cinder, or white dwarf, the size of the Earth. Over several million years the white dwarf will cool to a dim red dwarf, then a frozen, lightless black dwarf.

Life history of the Sun

 Life on Earth

The time from the birth of the Sun to the present has been divided into 12 "months" (below). In another 12 "months," the Sun will have used up all of the hydrogen that was in its core and will begin to die.

| 1 | 2 | 3 | 4 | 5 |

6

7

8

9

10

Microorganisms appear

1 12 11

Multicellular animals appear

Fish appear

Trees appear

Dinosaurs appear

Dinosaurs become extinct

Humans appear

2

3

4

5

6

7

8

9

10

11

12

1

2

3

4

5

Birth of the Sun
Surface temperature:
3,800° K.
Brightness: 100 to
1,000 times that of
today's Sun
Diameter: 50 times
that of today's Sun
Core temperature:
15,000° K.

The Sun today
Surface temperature:
6,000° K.
Diameter:
864,950 miles
Core temperature:
15 million° K.

7 billion years
from now. With
most of the hydro-
gen gone, the nu-
clear fires ebb. The
core collapses un-
der its own weight.
Heat from the con-
traction puffs out
the Sun to the size
of a red giant.

From giant to
dwarf. With no hy-
drogen left, the red
giant phase ends.
The remaining heli-
um begins an ex-
plosive fusion flash,
destroying the
Sun's outer layers.

Red giant
Surface temperature:
3,500° K.
Brightness: 100 to 500
times that of today's Sun
Diameter: 100 to 400
times that of today's Sun

6

7

8

White dwarf
Surface temperature:
7,000° K.
Mass: Half the mass of
today's Sun
Diameter: 1% of
today's Sun
Brightness: 1,000 times
dimmer than today's Sun

Red dwarf

A white dwarf.
Without the outer
layers, only an in-
credibly dense core
is left. The Sun is a
white dwarf.

The dwarf has
cooled to red. It is
about to become a
frozen black dwarf.

How Does the Sun Affect the Earth?

Although only a tiny fraction of the Sun's radiation reaches our planet, the Sun affects every aspect of life on Earth. An average of 123 watts falls on each square foot of the outer atmosphere per second, little more energy than a bright light bulb supplies. The total amount that falls per second equals the energy produced by burning 7 million tons of coal a second. Solar energy powers weather, air, and water circulation, and all life on Earth. Less noticeable is the Sun's occasional flashy activity, its flares and solar wind that interrupt communications and electricity and provide dazzling auroras, when electrically charged particles enter Earth's atmosphere.

Leaves bathed in sunlight produce carbohydrates through photosynthesis.

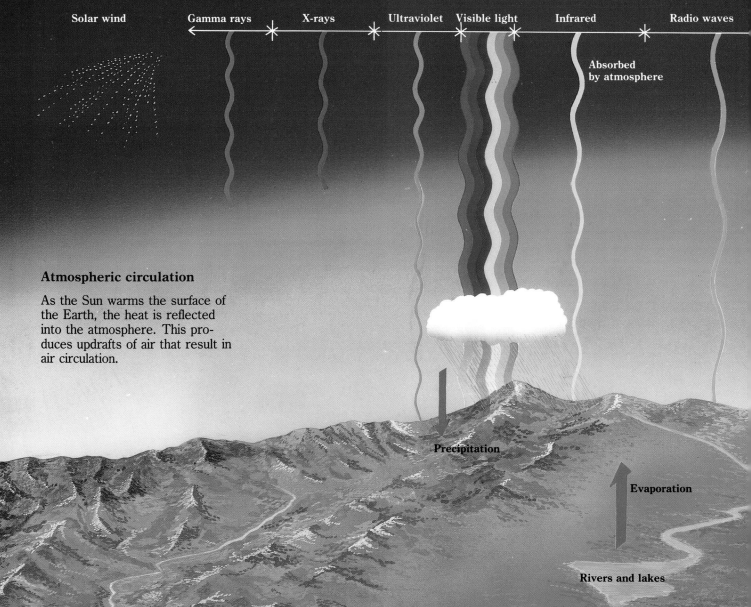

Solar wind · Gamma rays · X-rays · Ultraviolet · Visible light · Infrared · Radio waves

Absorbed by atmosphere

Atmospheric circulation

As the Sun warms the surface of the Earth, the heat is reflected into the atmosphere. This produces updrafts of air that result in air circulation.

Precipitation

Evaporation

Rivers and lakes

Radio interference

Solar wind pours into Earth's atmosphere, disturbing power and communications systems.

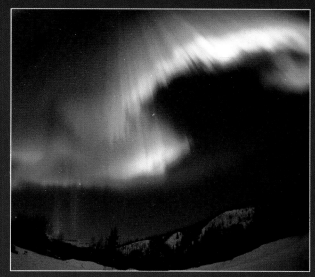

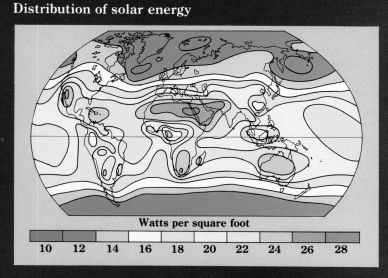

Distribution of solar energy

Watts per square foot

| 10 | 12 | 14 | 16 | 18 | 20 | 22 | 24 | 26 | 28 |

A shimmering aurora over Norway manifests the solar wind's interference at the North Pole.

Solar energy reaching the atmosphere—100%

Energy used in moving the atmosphere—0.002%

Energy used in moving water—23%

Energy used in photosynthesis—0.0002%

Energy warming the atmosphere, land, and water—47%

Directly reflected by the atmosphere —30%

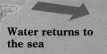

Wind

Water circulation

Earth's surface water, warmed by the Sun, evaporates and rises with the air. When the clouds cool, they drop the moisture as rain.

Sunlight reaches Earth unevenly, as shown in the map above. Areas just north of the equator—where high pressure reduces cloud cover—receive most of the Sun's rays *(dark pink)*. Sunlight falls off sharply near the poles.

Flow of solar energy

The thinnest outer veil of Earth's atmosphere feels the gamut of solar wavelengths, from gamma rays to radio waves. High-energy gamma rays and x-rays hit atoms and lose energy in an atmospheric layer above 50 miles. At 30 miles high, short wavelength ultraviolet light—dangerous to living things—collides with ozone molecules. Clouds, dust, and air pollutants absorb and scatter some of the remaining light, coloring the sky blue. Only light in the visible spectrum, some infrared and radio waves, plus a tiny fraction of longer wave ultraviolet rays, ever reach the surface.

Plants cover many land surfaces

Water returns to the sea

Ocean currents

Sea water circulates from the warm equatorial regions to the cool polar regions.

Photosynthetic organisms

Plants, algae, and some bacteria use solar energy to convert carbon dioxide and water into sugar molecules, beginning a food chain that leads to all living beings.

49

3

The Motion of the Earth

Standing on the Moon in 1969, humans first saw their home planet shining like a blue-and-white marble spinning through the blackness of space. Having successfully piloted a spaceship using calculations of planetary movement, the astronauts did not question that the Earth spun on its axis, that the Moon circled it, and that both bodies circled the Sun in an endless waltz.

These motions, however, were not obvious to thinkers in days gone by. After all, to the average observer the Sun appears to rise in the east and set in the west. The stars, too, rise and set every night. Early people quite sensibly believed that the universe circled around a stationary Earth. Only gradually, over the centuries, did astronomers who were both careful observers and bold theorists come to change public opinion. Scientists such as Nicolaus Copernicus, Jean-Bernard-Léon Foucault, and Friedrich Bessel showed that the Earth circled the Sun, tilted on its axis and spinning as it flew.

In order to study this motion, astronomers have relied on a "celestial sphere," a system of mapping the space around the Earth. At the center of the sphere is the Earth; the Earth's equator extends out to be the celestial equator, and lines of latitude and longitude crisscross the sphere of the sky just as they do a globe of the Earth. Stars and constellations can be mapped on this imaginary grid, as can the relative motions of the Sun, Moon, and Earth. So, too, can the awe-inspiring occasions known as eclipses.

Eclipsed by the disk of the Moon, the Sun displays its outer halo of hot gases. Between one and four solar eclipses occur each year; each one is visible only to a certain area on Earth.

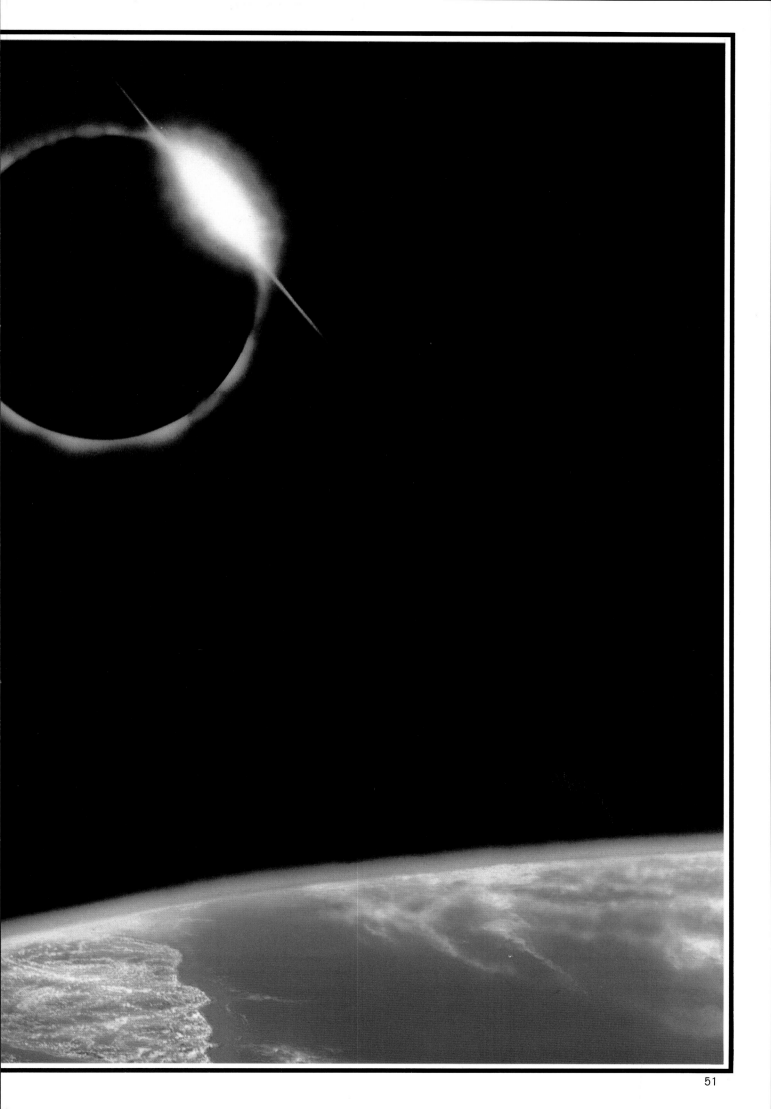

How Do We Know the Earth Rotates?

Until the sixteenth century, most people believed that the Sun circled around the Earth. But in 1543, the great Polish astronomer Nicolaus Copernicus published a radical theory that claimed the Earth circled the Sun, turning (rotating) on its axis to create night and day.

The Earth's rotation was hard to prove, however. Then, in 1851, a French physicist named Jean-Bernard-Léon Foucault hung a heavy iron ball on a wire from a tall ceiling. He knew that if the Earth did *not* rotate, the pendulum would swing back and forth over the same line. But if the Earth was turning, the pendulum's path would change. This is what happened. The Earth rotated under the free-swinging pendulum.

Because the Earth rotates, stars in the northern sky appear to circle Polaris.

Foucault's pendulum

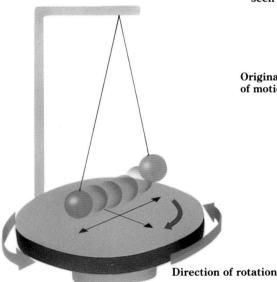

Direction of rotation

To prove the Earth turns, Foucault devised an ingenious experiment. If he couldn't leave the planet to watch it move, perhaps he could make a device that moved independently of the planet. So he hung a 62-pound iron ball from the 220-foot-high ceiling of a building in Paris. A special attachment ensured that the wire would swing smoothly. Under the weight sat a pan of sand.

When Foucault swung the pendulum, a needle on the weight traced a line in the sand. Each hour, Foucault found the line had changed direction slightly, until the pendulum retraced its original path. The motion of the pendulum kept it swinging along the same line, but the Earth and the building attached to the Earth had rotated under it. If Foucault had been able to ride his pendulum, he might have seen the room turn slowly around him.

A ball's motion seen from above

Original plane of motion

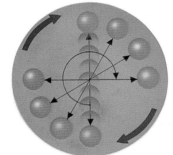

A pendulum at the North Pole would swing clockwise once every 24 hours.

At a latitude between pole and equator, the pendulum circles every 30 hours.

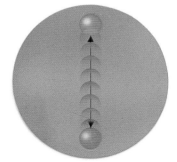

At the equator, the pendulum swings back and forth along a single plane.

Pendulum in middle latitudes

Pendulum at equator

The Coriolis force

If you tried bowling on a stationary merry-go-round, you could hit the pins. But if the merry-go-round rotated, you'd have trouble. By the time the ball had traveled the distance, the pins would have moved to the left with the merry-go-round. It would seem as if something had pushed your ball to the right. Scientists call this apparent force the Coriolis force.

Stationary disk

Path seen from above

Rotating disk

The Coriolis force on Earth

The Coriolis force pushes cyclones from the equator to the right in the Northern Hemisphere and to the left in the Southern.

Pendulum at North Pole

Traveling stars

Like the Sun, stars appear to travel across the heavens, rising in the east and setting in the west. But these starry arcs are a result of the Earth's rotation under a relatively unchanging sky.

Sky overhead

At the North Pole, stars seem to draw counterclockwise concentric circles around Polaris.

Sky overhead

Mid-latitude

At middle latitudes, most stars appear to rise in the east and set in the west. A few stars still circle the pole.

Sky overhead

Equator

Near the equator, all stars appear to rise and set. They seem to follow a track perpendicular to the horizon.

What Is the Earth's Orbit?

Ancient astronomers observed that different stars and planets appeared in Earth's night sky during the year. They thought this was because the stars, as well as the Sun, circled the Earth. After Copernicus, when this theory came into doubt, it was still difficult to prove that the Earth itself was moving.

In 1838, the German astronomer Friedrich Bessel, using a telescope, showed that some stars appeared to shift their position relative to other stars. This proved that those stars were closer to the Earth than others in the background and that the Earth itself was in motion.

As the Earth swings through space, the constellation Orion seems to trek across the sky, changing location from month to month.

The ecliptic

Because the Earth orbits the Sun, a line of sight from Earth through the Sun will point to a different part of the sky each month. As the Earth travels from E1 to E2 *(left)*, the Sun appears to travel from S1 to S2. We can't see the starry backdrop behind the bright Sun, but we can look in the opposite direction at night. The constellations we see in July will lie directly behind the Sun in December.

Twelve constellations lie in the plane apparently traced by the Sun. This plane, called the ecliptic, *(marked left and below in orange)* is actually the orbital plane of the Earth.

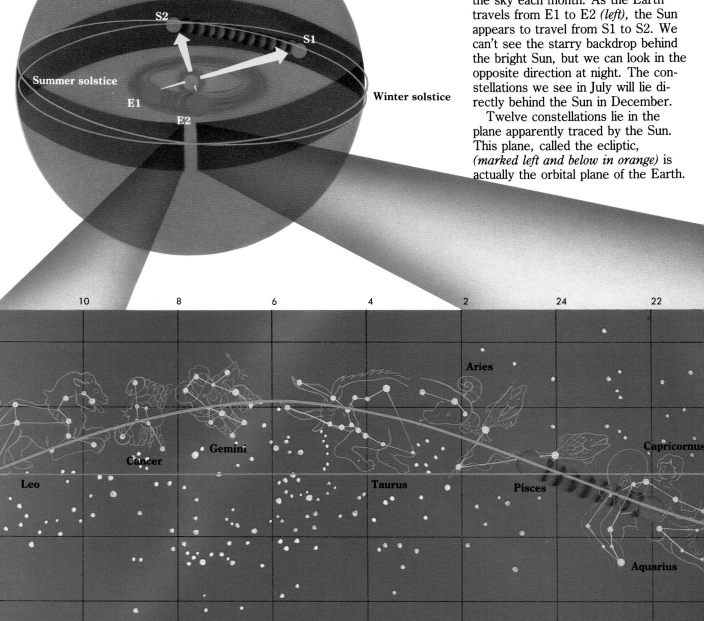

Parallax

As the Earth moves through space, the positions of nearby stars appear to shift relative to the vastly distant stellar backdrop. This effect, called parallax, also occurs if you watch your finger and a more distant object while waggling your head from side to side. The nearer the star is to Earth, the larger the parallax. Stars on the same orbital plane (ecliptic) as the Earth appear to move back and forth; those directly perpendicular to the ecliptic seem to move in a circle; and those that are in-between trace out an oval.

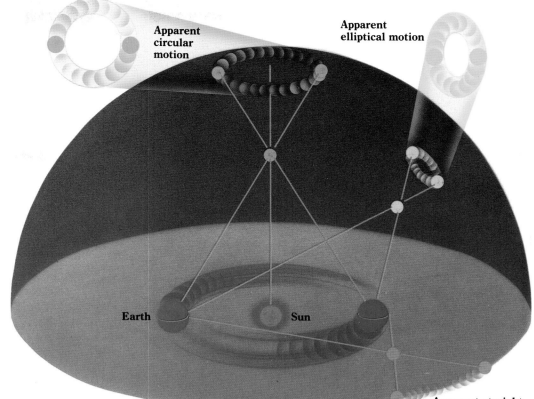

Apparent circular motion

Apparent elliptical motion

Earth

Sun

Apparent straight-line motion

Slanting starlight

Like rain falling to the ground, light from a star takes time to reach the Earth. Meanwhile, as the light travels, our planet is moving through space at 65,000 miles per hour. Imagine raindrops falling outside a train window. If the train is not moving, the rain appears to fall straight down. But if the train is speeding forward, the rain seems to fall at a slant. Starlight, too, seems to slant toward the Earth as the Earth moves, an effect called aberration of starlight. Because of this effect, stars appear to shift from their true positions over the course of a year. English astronomer James Bradley discovered this proof of Earth's motion in 1728, though some astronomers remained unconvinced for 110 years.

Stationary train

Moving train

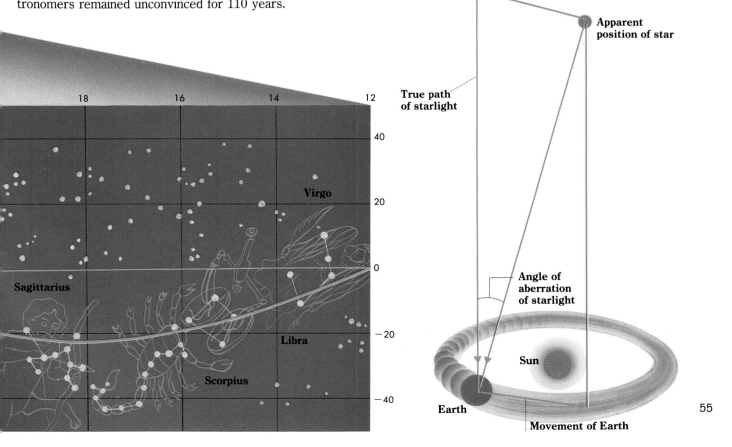

18   16   14   12

40

20

Virgo

0

Sagittarius

−20

Libra

Scorpius

−40

True position of star

Apparent position of star

True path of starlight

Angle of aberration of starlight

Sun

Earth

Movement of Earth

55

Why Are There Seasons?

If the Earth did not tilt on its axis, there would be no seasons. Every day would have 12 hours of light and 12 of dark. But since the planet's axis is at an angle to its orbital plane, we have summer and winter, long days and short.

The 23.45° tilt between the equator and the orbital plane causes each hemisphere to lean toward the Sun for part of the year. When the North Pole tips toward the Sun, the Northern Hemisphere basks in summer warmth. Six months later, the Earth has swung through half its orbit. Now the South Pole angles toward the Sun. Australia has summer and North America shivers.

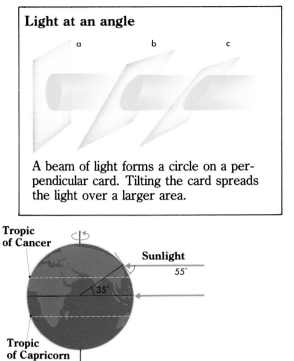

Light at an angle

A beam of light forms a circle on a perpendicular card. Tilting the card spreads the light over a larger area.

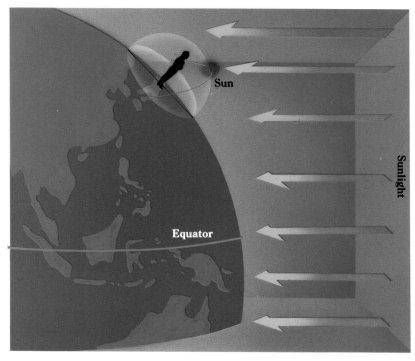

Vernal equinox

An equinox occurs each spring and fall when the Earth's rotational axis is perpendicular to the Sun's rays *(above and left)*. To someone who is standing at 35° latitude, the Sun at the spring, or vernal, equinox shines on the Earth at an angle of about 55°.

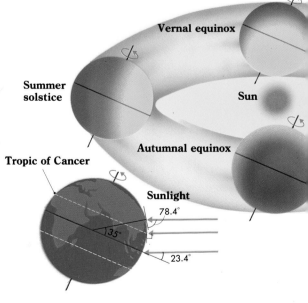

Summer solstice

About June 22, the North Pole slants most toward the Sun *(above and left)*. This day is the summer solstice. On Earth, the Sun appears to reach its northernmost point, shining vertically on 23.4° north latitude, the Tropic of Cancer. At 35° latitude in the United States and Asia, the Sun's angle reaches 78.4°.

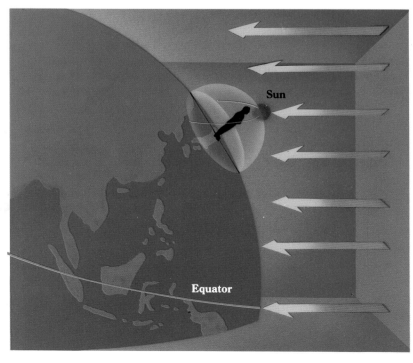

Daylight hours

The Earth's swing around the Sun exposes different parts of its surface to sunlight for different lengths of time each day. Near the summer solstice in the Northern Hemisphere, the Sun appears to spend more time above the horizon than below it. At the same time of year in the Southern Hemisphere, nights are longer than days. Around the winter solstice in the Northern Hemisphere, the Sun's arc seems lower and shorter. With fewer hours of daylight, the Earth receives less heat. The illustration at right graphs sunlight that accumulates throughout the year at a middle northern latitude.

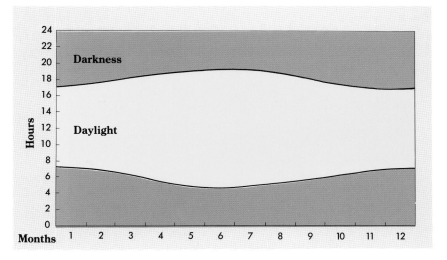

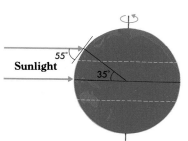

Autumnal equinox

During the autumnal equinox, day and night again become equal. The Sun shines vertically over the equator and at an angle north and south of the equator *(above and right)*. These areas receive less heat because the solar radiation is spread over a larger area.

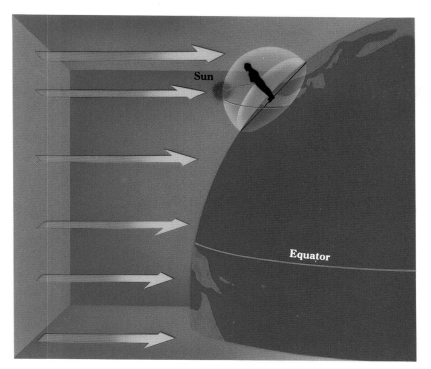

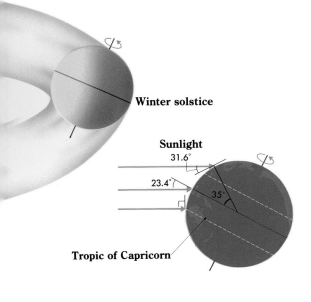

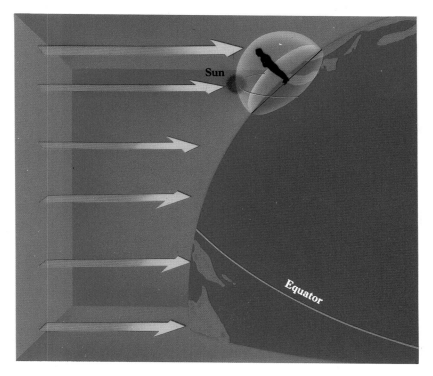

Winter solstice

At the winter solstice, December 22, the Sun shines vertically on the Tropic of Capricorn at 23.4° south latitude. The Sun's light slants toward the United States and Asia at a low 31.6°. This is the Northern Hemisphere's shortest day.

Where Does the Midnight Sun Shine?

Because the Earth's axis tilts, the area near its poles stays constantly in the sunlight during each hemisphere's midsummer. This land of the midnight Sun—which includes some of Alaska, Scandinavia, and the Soviet Union in the Northern Hemisphere—swings in a circle as the Earth turns on its axis. But the circle is so small that these places never rotate out of the Sun's light. The Sun appears to sink toward the horizon, but stays visible all night. In the Northern Hemisphere, this takes place in June. In Antarctica, surrounding the South Pole, the Sun shines all night during the southern summer, late in December.

Even at ten o'clock at night, the summer sun shines brightly on this Norwegian town.

● **Arctic summer**

To someone standing on the Arctic Circle on the summer solstice, June 22, the Sun never completely sets but merely skims the horizon.

■ **Summer solstice in the Arctic**

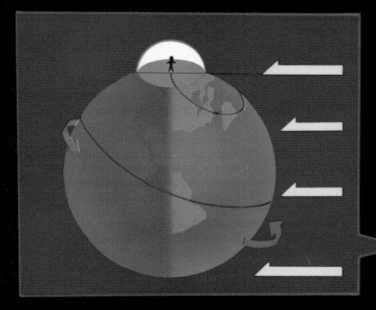

Sun at midnight

The Sun's apparent path changes at different latitudes. The illustration at right shows the Sun's path near the equator *(blue line)*, at two northern latitudes *(green lines)*, and at the pole *(pink line)*. The Sun traces a similar path in the Southern Hemisphere at the summer solstice *(below, left)*. In either hemisphere, the Sun never sinks below the horizon above 66.5° latitude.

● **Southern summer**

● **Northern summer**

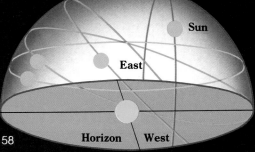

Sun

East

Horizon   West

Sun   East

Earth

West   Horizon

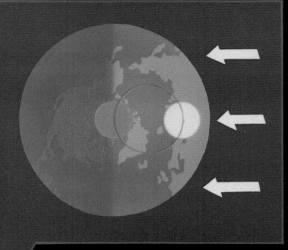

● The Sun's path

At the North Pole, day and night each seem six months long. During the summer solstice, the Sun circles parallel to the horizon, but 23.5° up. At both equinoxes, it circles at the horizon. And during the six-month winter, the Sun disappears, circling as low as 23.5° below the horizon at the winter solstice.

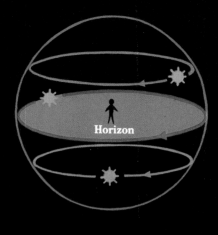

Horizon

● The Arctic Circle

From far above the North Pole at the summer solstice, half the Earth would appear lit by the Sun and half would remain dark. The Arctic Circle would lie entirely in the sunlit half.

Sun at noon

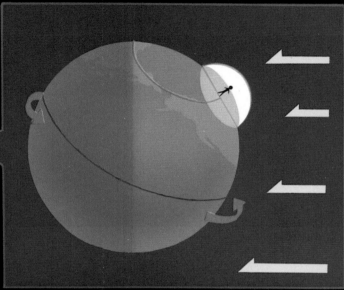

● High noon

At the summer solstice on the Arctic Circle, the noon Sun reaches 47° into the sky. After the solstice, the Sun slips lower each day until it reaches the horizon.

In this multiple-exposure photograph near the Arctic Circle, the Sun drops to skim the horizon at midnight, then rises again.

What Is the North Star?

Because the Earth is not perfectly round—it bulges out about 27 miles at the equator—the gravity of the Sun and Moon tugs at the planet as it spins on its axis. This makes the Earth wobble very slowly, so that its poles gradually trace out a circle in space.

This motion is called precession, and it takes about 26,000 years for a single circle to be completed. Meanwhile, the North Pole will point to new "north stars." Today, the North Pole points toward a star called Polaris. But 8,000 years in the future, it will point toward the next bright North Star, Deneb in the Swan constellation.

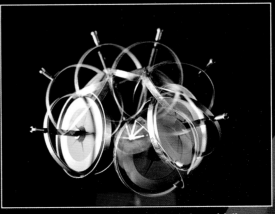

The combination of gravity and a whirling, circular weight keeps the axis of a gyroscope —or a planet—moving in a broad cone.

● **The tug of gravity**

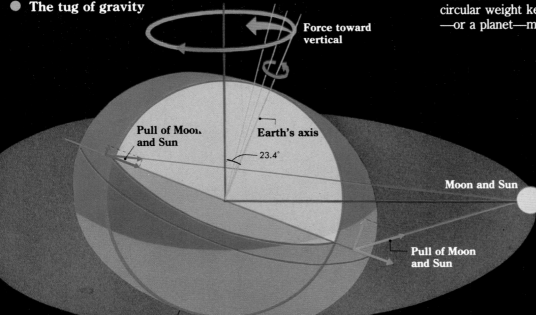

Force toward vertical

Pull of Moon and Sun

Earth's axis

23.4°

Moon and Sun

Pull of Moon and Sun

Two opposing forces tug the Earth into its wobble. The first is the planet's spin, which keeps it tilted on its axis. The second force is the gravitational pull of both the Sun and the Moon, which tries to straighten up the tilt of the Earth.

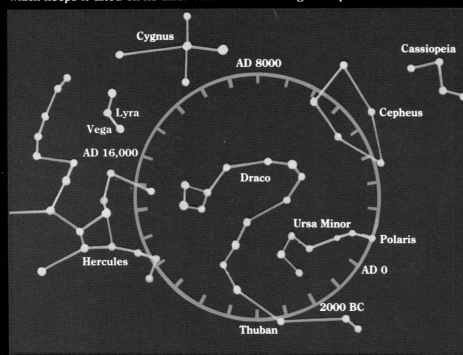

Cygnus

AD 8000

Cassiopeia

Lyra

Cepheus

Vega

AD 16,000

Draco

Ursa Minor

Polaris

Hercules

AD 0

2000 BC

Thuban

● **New north stars**

Precession causes a cycle of north stars that lasts about 26,000 years. The North Pole will pass Polaris in a few hundred years and head for the constellation Cepheus. The next North Star will lie in Cygnus, the Swan, followed in AD 14,000 by the star Vega.

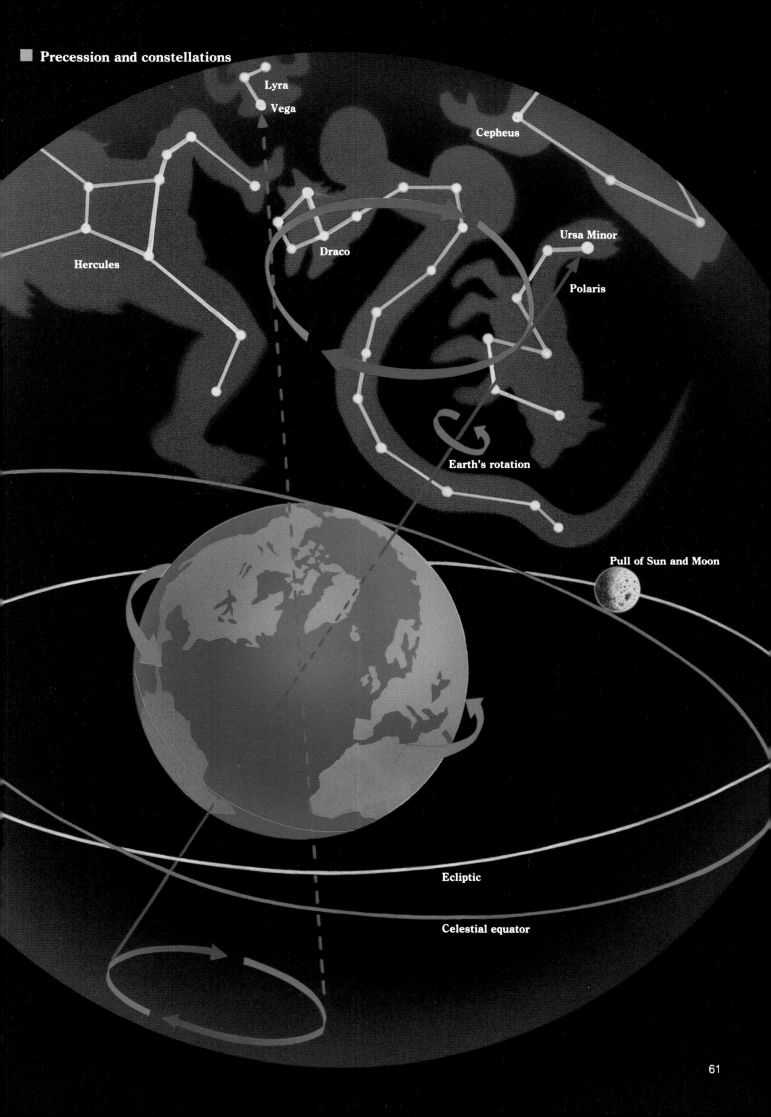

Lyra

Vega

Cepheus

Draco

Hercules

Ursa Minor

Polaris

Earth's rotation

Pull of Sun and Moon

Ecliptic

Celestial equator

What Causes Eclipses?

On a normal night, the Moon shines gently with reflected sunlight. But when the Earth passes exactly between the Sun and Moon, the Earth's shadow falls on its satellite. This causes a lunar eclipse, in which the Moon seems to fade to darkness. On the other hand, when the Moon moves exactly between the Earth and the Sun, a small Moon shadow falls on Earth. Observers who are in that shadow will be able to see a solar eclipse, which occurs when the Sun disappears behind the Moon's disk.

Eclipses occur regularly and with great variety. Because of the way the Sun's rays spread out, both the Earth and the Moon cast a dark shadow (the umbra) inside a lighter shadow (the penumbra). If the Moon swings into the Earth's umbra, a total lunar eclipse takes place; the Earth's penumbra darkens the Moon only slightly. During a solar eclipse, only observers within the umbra see a total eclipse, which may entirely hide the Sun or else leave a thin, bright ring of light around the Moon's dark disk.

Lunar eclipse

Sun

Solar eclipse

Moon

When eclipses occur

Every month, the Moon swings from the Sun side of Earth (new moon) to the opposite side (full moon) and back. So why isn't there one solar and one lunar eclipse each month? Because the Moon's orbital plane tilts about 5° away from the Earth's and the lunar orbit varies, the Moon seldom crosses the Earth's orbital plane between Sun and Earth.

Sun

Moon

Earth

Celestial equator

Total lunar eclipse

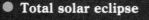

In a total lunar eclipse, when the Moon's orbit carries it into the umbra of the Earth's shadow, no sunlight shines on the Moon. But it does not appear black. The Earth's atmosphere bends and scatters some sunlight, and the Moon takes on the color of hot copper.

Total solar eclipse

Penumbra

Partial solar eclipse

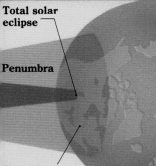

Total solar eclipse

A total solar eclipse begins when the Moon swings between the Sun and Earth. If the Moon's oval orbit has carried it far from Earth, it will seem too small to cover the Sun and a ring of light will appear around the Moon's edge. This is an annular eclipse. If the Moon is close to Earth, its disk will completely cover the Sun. Seen from space, a Moon shadow 167 miles wide races across the globe at about 1,000 miles per hour.

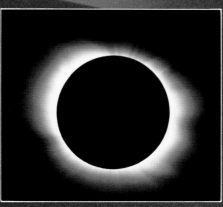

Total solar eclipse

Annular eclipse

Partial solar eclipse

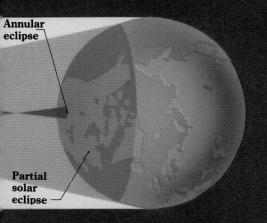

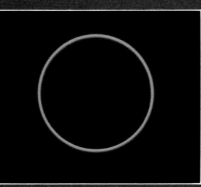

Annular eclipse

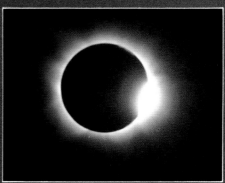

Diamond-ring effect

4
The Moon

Since ancient times, people have been fascinated by the mysteries of the Moon. They have told imaginative stories in attempts to explain what the Moon is and how it was born. Some people thought they could see familiar shapes, such as rabbits and old women, in the random patterns of the lunar surface. Only in recent times have telescopes and spaceflights revealed the true face of the Moon, a desolate, crater-pocked landscape of mountains and vast basins of lava, known as *maria* (Latin for "seas") because they were once thought to be true oceans. Craters, ranging from the size of potholes to huge impact basins hundreds of miles across, dominate the lunar surface. With no significant atmosphere to burn up falling meteorites and asteroids, the Moon preserves a four-billion-year record of cosmic violence. Scientists disagree on how the Moon originated, and no one is sure whether it formed together with Earth, broke off from Earth after a collision with another body, or formed elsewhere and was later captured by Earth's gravity. Whatever its origin, today the Moon is geologically inactive as the seismographs left behind by the Apollo astronauts showed. Only one-fourth the diameter of Earth, with just 1.25 percent of its mass, the Moon is a captive of Earth's gravitational force. Because it rotates only once around its axis while it completes one orbit around the Earth, the Moon always presents the same face to Earth; but the Moon's gravitational force is still strong enough to control ocean tides on Earth.

Cosmic debris, ranging from rock size to bodies several hundred miles in diameter, crashed on the Moon early in its history and throughout its four billion years, forming thousands of craters, which now dominate the lunar surface.

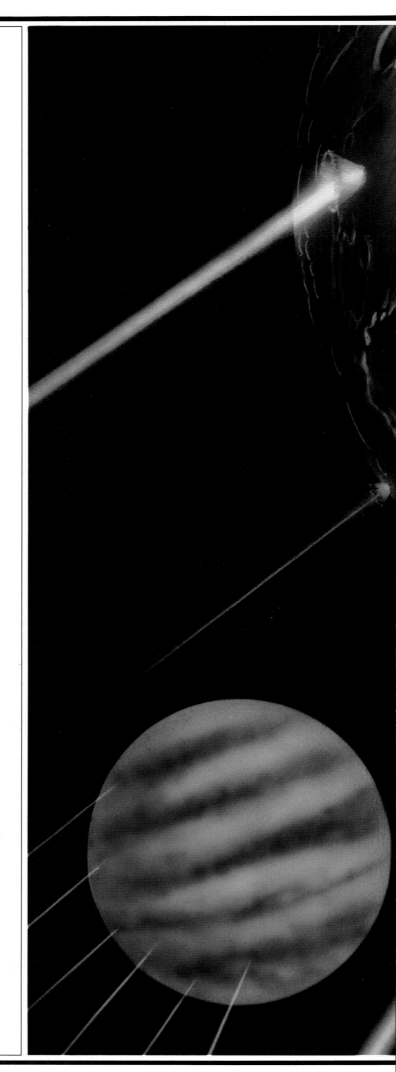

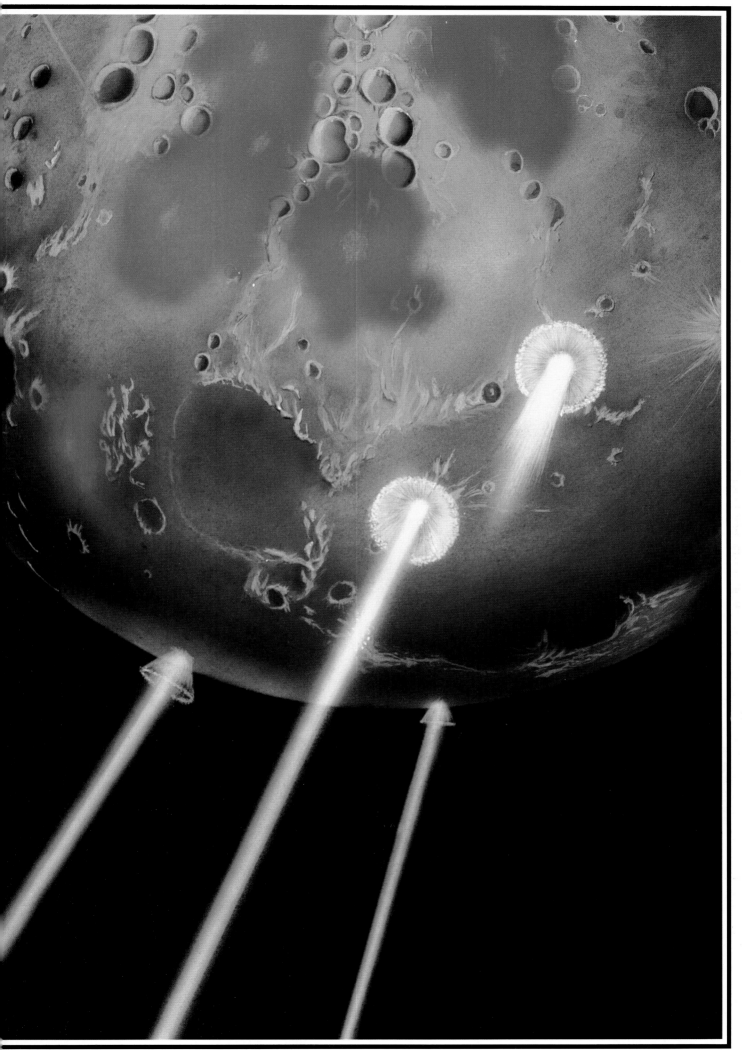

How Did the Moon Form?

When the Sun was born at the center of a collapsing nebula, gas and dust coalesced into rocky bodies known as planetesimals. The proto-Earth formed in the midst of a solar system churning with debris. One theory suggests that soon after its formation, the proto-Earth was struck by a planetesimal about the size of Mars. The collision melted Earth's outer layers of rock and threw off huge clouds of material that settled into orbit around the young planet. Within a few thousand years, gravity drew the debris together, forming the proto-Moon.

Proto-Earth

2 A fiery impact

The high-speed collision melted Earth's mantle; low-density rock was blown off the surface.

Planetesimal

1 A cosmic collision

A large body may have struck Earth soon after the formation of the Solar System in an area where a multitude of planetesimals orbited the Sun.

Earth

Proto-Moon

4 Birth of the Moon
Gravitational forces quickly pulled the ring of debris together, forming planetesimals that coalesced into the proto-Moon.

3 A ring of debris
Dust and gas dispersed by the collision were gripped by Earth's gravity. The debris settled into orbiting rings.

Earthrise. The Earth, with its bountiful oceans and cloud-draped skies—as seen from the Moon—presents a stark contrast to the dry and airless Moon.

● **A trio of theories**

Many scientists think the collision theory best explains the Moon's origin, but some hold different views. The "sister theory" *(top right)* proposes that the Earth and the Moon formed separately, but at about the same time and place. The "fission theory" *(middle right)* suggests that the rapidly spinning proto-Earth fragmented and split apart, and the liberated blob of hot matter became the Moon. The "capture theory" *(bottom right)* sets forth that the Moon formed elsewhere in the Solar System and was later captured by the stronger gravitational pull of Earth. Each theory has its strengths and weaknesses. Although the collision theory now seems the most persuasive, conclusive proof has not yet been found.

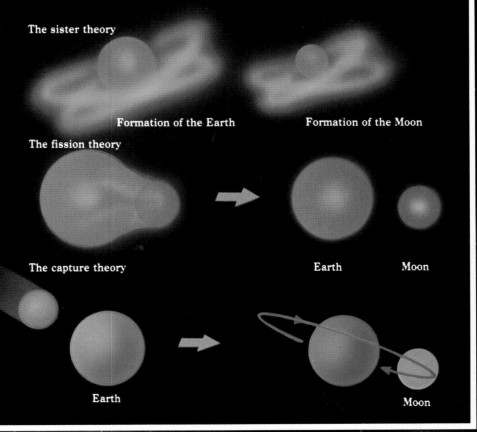

The sister theory

Formation of the Earth   Formation of the Moon

The fission theory

Earth   Moon

The capture theory

Earth

Moon

How Were the Moon's Craters and Seas Formed?

The newly formed Moon was a hot ball of liquid rock, known as magma. As the magma slowly cooled, the denser rock sank to form the Moon's core, while the lighter rock formed its mantle and thin crust. By about four billion years ago, the surface crust had solidified, although it was still being blasted by the impact of planetesimals. Over the next 500 million years, such collisions became less frequent. Meanwhile, hot liquid magma flowed out of the interior and filled the surface depressions caused by the impacts. The magma cooled, creating the basins of dark basalt that were once thought to be seas. Cratering continued at a slower rate, resulting in the lunar surface we see today.

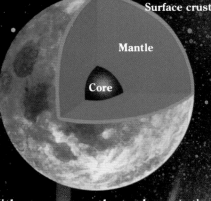

With a core, mantle, and crust, the Moon is 2,160 miles in diameter.

Magma

Crater

Crust

Mantle

1 An ocean of magma

When the Moon formed, molten magma covered its surface. As the magma cooled, the denser rock sank to the core; the lighter rock formed the crust.

2 A battered surface

As the crust cooled to form rock, thousands of impacts blasted craters in the surface.

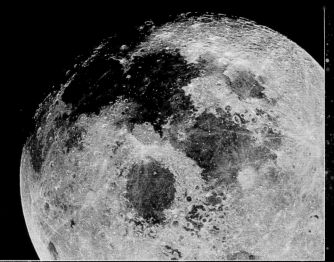

The view from _Apollo 11_. The dark lunar "seas" are basins of basalt that flowed from the Moon's interior.

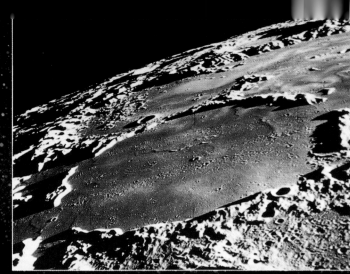

Ancient craters. Astronauts saw the surface from close up. The largest crater is 120 miles across.

Magma

3 Heat from below

Although the Moon's surface had cooled after a billion years, the interior was still hot, causing fluid magma in the mantle to rise toward the surface.

4 Filling the craters

Fewer impacts occurred after the first billion years of the Solar System's history. The craters filled with hot magma flowing up through the surface cracks.

5 Birth of the maria

The hot magma overflowed the craters and spread across the vast lowland basins. The largest such basin, Imbrium, is 780 miles across. The magma cooled to form dark basaltic rock. Finally, the interior cooled, and the magma flow ended about 2.5 billion years ago.

Why Is Only One Side of the Moon Visible from Earth?

Although the phases of the Moon—from new moon to full moon—are constantly changing, its face remains the same. Seen from Earth, Mare Crisium is always near the eastern rim and the great Tycho crater is always near the center of the southern hemisphere. Because it is subject to Earth's tidal forces, the Moon's rotation around its axis has slowed to match its revolution around Earth. The Moon takes 27.3 days to orbit Earth and 27.3 days to rotate around its axis. This "synchronous rotation" means one side of the Moon always faces Earth and the other always faces away.

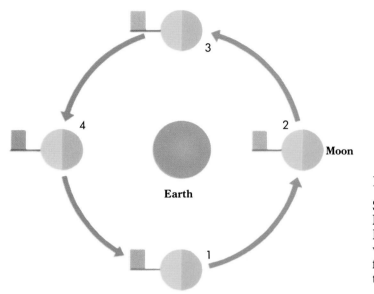

The motion of the Moon. The Moon's orbit around Earth is tilted 5°9′ relative to the Sun's path on the "celestial sphere," known as the ecliptic. The Moon crosses the ecliptic at the ascending and descending nodes.

Does the Moon rotate?

Suppose the Moon did *not* rotate. Then, a flagpole on the Moon's surface *(left)* would always point in one direction. But as the Moon revolved around the Earth, observers would see the flag from different angles. Just as the visible face of the flag would change, so would the visible face of the Moon, allowing us to see both sides instead of one.

Synchronous rotation

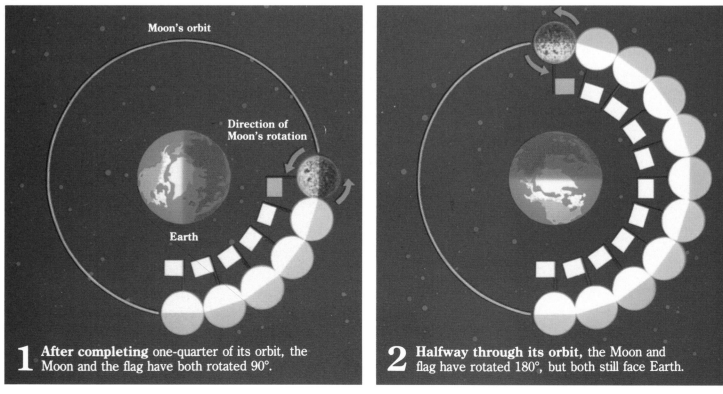

1 **After completing** one-quarter of its orbit, the Moon and the flag have both rotated 90°.

2 **Halfway through its orbit,** the Moon and flag have rotated 180°, but both still face Earth.

Can we see the Moon's far side?

Although it is true that the Moon always presents the same face to Earth, it is still possible to get a glimpse of its far side. The Moon's orbit around the Earth is not a perfect circle, but rather an ellipse. As it follows this ellipse, the Moon moves slightly faster during the times when it is closest to Earth. At those periods, its rate of revolution and rate of rotation are slightly out of phase with each other, so that seen from Earth, the Moon seems to wobble slightly. This wobble, known as libration, allows observers on Earth to see part of the Moon's far side. In all, we can see 59 percent of the Moon's surface from Earth, but we can never see more than 50 percent of it at any one time. The remaining 41 percent can never be seen from Earth.

The Moon's elliptical orbit

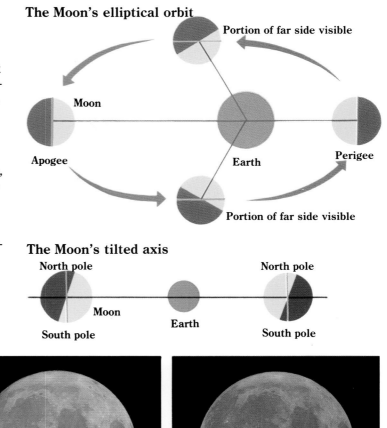

The Moon's tilted axis

A view of 50% of the Moon

The eastern rim

The western rim

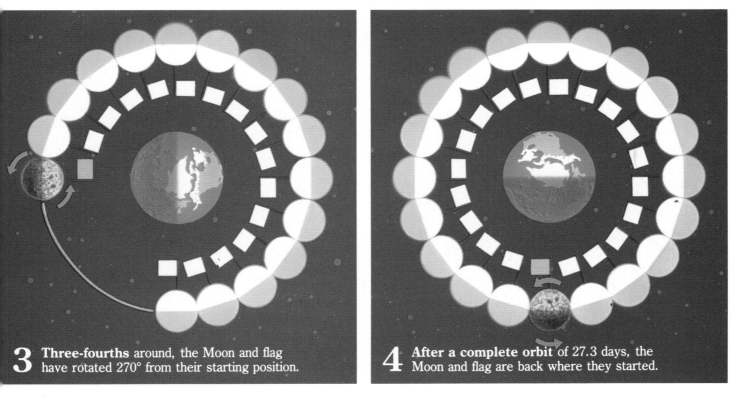

3 **Three-fourths** around, the Moon and flag have rotated 270° from their starting position.

4 **After a complete orbit** of 27.3 days, the Moon and flag are back where they started.

Is the Moon Receding from Earth?

Every year, the Moon moves a little farther away from Earth—but only a very short distance. Precise measurements show that the Moon is receding from Earth at a rate of 1.2 inches per year. In a million years, the Moon will have moved about 18 miles farther out.

According to the collision theory, the Moon originally formed much closer to the Earth than it is today, orbiting the planet at a distance of about 10,000 miles. If the theory is correct, then the Moon would have made revolutions around Earth much more quickly, in less than a day. But the tidal forces that were created by Earth's gravity acted as a brake on the Moon, gradually slowing down its orbital speed and rate of rotation. As the Moon's motion slowed, its orbit gradually expanded, until it reached its present radius of about 230,400 miles.

By measuring the time it takes for a laser beam to return to the Earth from reflectors on the Moon, very accurate measurements of distance can be made.

The receding Moon

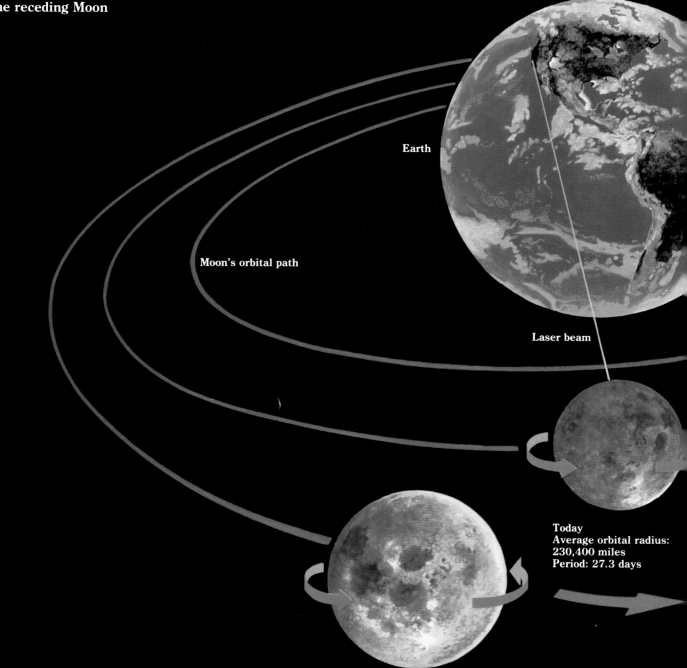

Earth

Moon's orbital path

Laser beam

Today
Average orbital radius: 230,400 miles
Period: 27.3 days

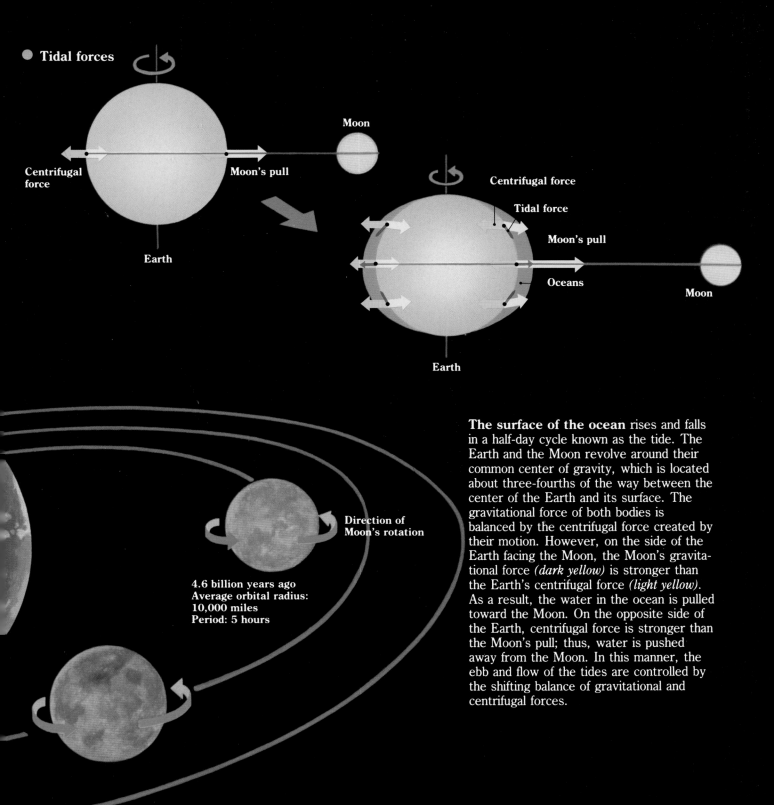

● **Tidal forces**

Centrifugal force

Moon's pull

Moon

Earth

Centrifugal force

Tidal force

Moon's pull

Oceans

Moon

Earth

Direction of Moon's rotation

**4.6 billion years ago
Average orbital radius:
10,000 miles
Period: 5 hours**

The surface of the ocean rises and falls in a half-day cycle known as the tide. The Earth and the Moon revolve around their common center of gravity, which is located about three-fourths of the way between the center of the Earth and its surface. The gravitational force of both bodies is balanced by the centrifugal force created by their motion. However, on the side of the Earth facing the Moon, the Moon's gravitational force *(dark yellow)* is stronger than the Earth's centrifugal force *(light yellow)*. As a result, the water in the ocean is pulled toward the Moon. On the opposite side of the Earth, centrifugal force is stronger than the Moon's pull; thus, water is pushed away from the Moon. In this manner, the ebb and flow of the tides are controlled by the shifting balance of gravitational and centrifugal forces.

High tides do not happen at the precise moment when a point on Earth is at its minimum distance from the Moon. Rather, there is a delay of two or three hours because of the force of friction. As the Earth rotates, it drags the water in the oceans along with it. Friction between the water and the ocean bottom slows the motion of both the water and the Earth. The ocean water swelling toward the Moon has greater force than the water pushed away from it on the opposite side of the Earth. This unequal distribution of force acts as a brake on the rotation of the Earth. Tidal action is very gradually slowing down Earth's rotation. Every 100,000 years, the length of the day increases by one second. As the rotation slows, the balance of forces between Earth and its Moon changes, and the Moon's centrifugal force becomes stronger relative to Earth's gravity, allowing the Moon to move farther away from Earth.

Could Humans Live on the Moon?

The Moon is a dead world—there is no air to breathe, no water to drink, no grass, no trees, no life of any kind. The temperature on the surface varies between 266°F. during the day and −200°F. during the two-week-long lunar night. Yet human beings—the 12 Apollo astronauts—have already made short visits to the Moon, and ambitious plans are being developed for the construction of permanent human bases on our nearest celestial neighbor. At first, people traveling and planning a visit to the Moon will have to bring all their food, water, and air with them from Earth, but eventually those necessities may be produced on the Moon itself. Someday, there may be entire cities on the Moon where thousands of people can live in comfort and safety.

■ **A home on the Moon**

A ride on a Moon buggy. In 1972, *Apollo 17* astronauts used this ungainly vehicle to explore the Moon's surface and gather rock samples.

A lunar landing

Communications antennas

Liquid oxygen and other necessities will be stored in huge tanks.

Lunar landing stage

A lunar observatory. Earth's atmosphere blocks our view of many celestial objects, but on the airless Moon, observatories will have a clear view.

Observation platform

Control center

The first living areas for the Moon base may be constructed from used rocket fuel tanks, dug into the surface rocks. There will not be much room and conditions will be difficult at first.

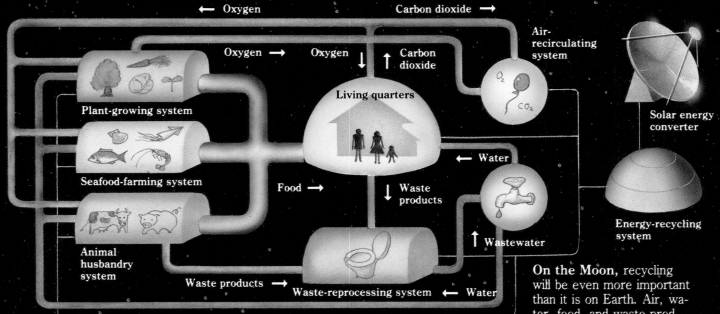

Oxygen ←   Carbon dioxide →

Oxygen →   Oxygen ↓   Carbon dioxide

Air-recirculating system

Plant-growing system

Living quarters

O₂ CO₂

Solar energy converter

Seafood-farming system

Oxygen ↓   Carbon dioxide ↑

← Water

Food →

↓ Waste products

↑ Wastewater

Animal husbandry system

Waste products →

Waste-reprocessing system   ← Water

Energy-recycling system

← Energy

On the Moon, recycling will be even more important than it is on Earth. Air, water, food, and waste products will be processed to provide the necessities of life. Food will be grown in greenhouses, where plants will use the carbon dioxide exhaled by humans and produce oxygen for breathing.

A factory will be set up to refine minerals found on the Moon, such as silicon, aluminum, and calcium oxide, used to make cement. Such building materials will not have to be sent up from Earth.

Because it will be expensive to ship rocket fuel to the Moon, a huge catapult may be built to fling cargo off the Moon toward a rendezvous with orbiting spacecraft.

🛰 **Lunar vehicle**

Concave mirrors will gather and focus solar energy to generate electricity for the Moon base.

Solar battery arrays will collect energy from the Sun during the two-week-long lunar day.

75

5
The Stars

At night, we see thousands of stars; during the day, we see only one: the nearby Sun. Other stars are trillions of miles away. In the interior of stars, at temperatures of millions of degrees, hydrogen atoms fuse to form helium nuclei and release energy. In stars much more massive than the Sun, nuclear fusion creates elements that are heavier than hydrogen and helium, such as carbon and oxygen. Elements heavier than iron are created when stars 10 times more massive than the Sun collapse upon their cores and explode in what are known as supernovas. A supernova briefly outshines all other stars in the galaxy, then dims. Eventually, only a small, very dense core remains, called a neutron star. Or, the supernova may have reduced the star to a point of infinite density, a black hole, from which nothing, not even light, can escape. Massive stars have relatively short lives, while stars like the Sun burn steadily for 10 billion years or more. Less massive stars burn less brightly but live even longer.

Stars are born when vast clouds of dust and gas collapse into concentrated whirlpools. A single cloud may spawn dozens of stars. As gravity concentrates the gas, temperature and pressure rise until nuclear reactions start and fuel the stars, which then emit heat and light. The rotating disk of dust and gas around a new star may contain all the elements needed to form planets. Our Sun, the Earth and its people are composed of elements once created in the centers of ancient stars and supernovas.

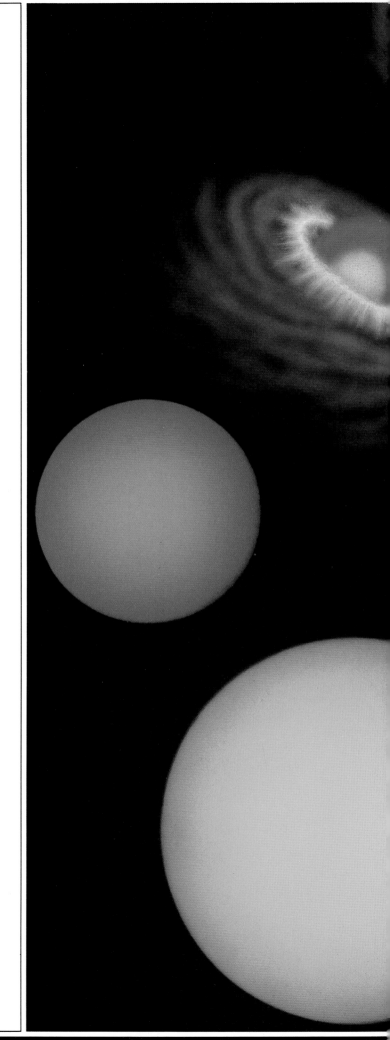

A huge cloud of gas and dust has spawned clumps and whirlpools that condense into newborn stars.

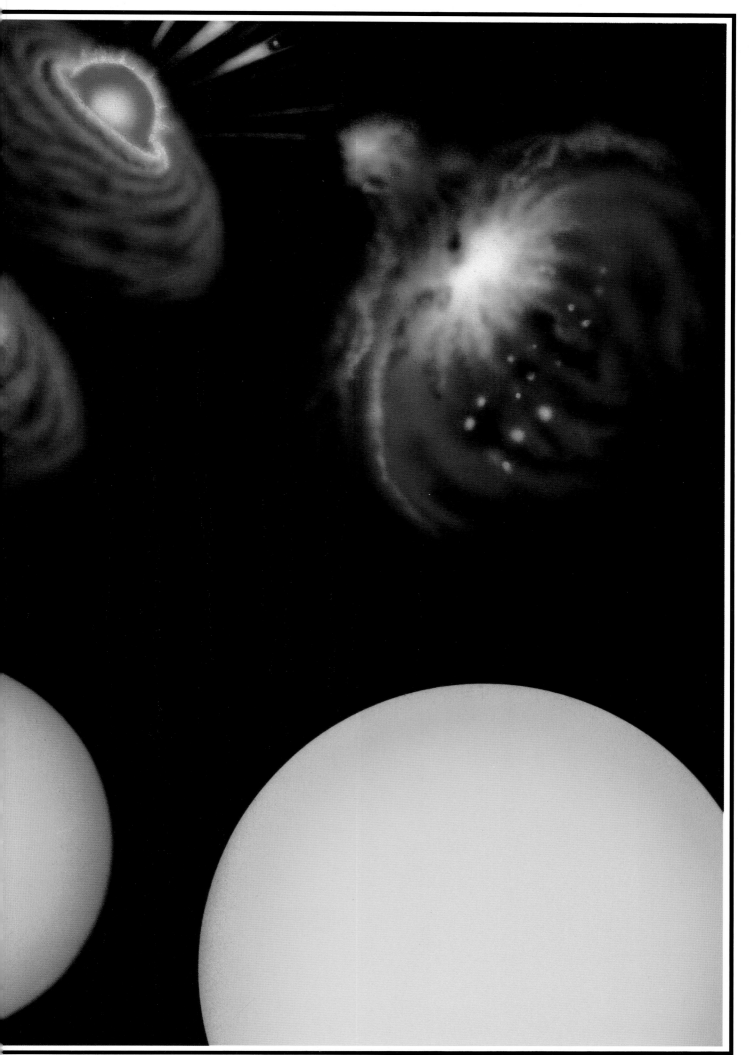

Why Do Stars Have Colors?

In the constellation Orion is one bright red star, Betelgeuse, and one bright blue star, Rigel; the others are mostly white stars. Stars shine in different colors because they have different mass, burn at different temperatures, and are made of different elements. To analyze the colors, astronomers use a spectrograph, which spreads out starlight the way rain diffuses sunlight to form a rainbow. Stellar rainbows, called spectra, contain dark lines known as absorption lines, caused by elements in the atmosphere of the star. By reading a star's spectrum, astronomers can tell how hot it is and what it is made of.

● Reading a star's spectrum

When light passes through a prism, it spreads out into a continuous rainbow of colors *(top right)*. Gases in the outer atmospheric layers of stars absorb certain wavelengths of light, leaving narrow gaps, or dark lines, in the stellar spectrum *(top center)*. Each element absorbs light at particular wavelengths. In a similar manner, gases at extremely high temperatures may also produce light at certain wavelengths, creating bright emission lines *(top, lower right)*. By reading the combination of bright or dark lines in the spectrum of a star, astronomers are able to tell which particular elements are present in the star and what the temperature is at its surface.

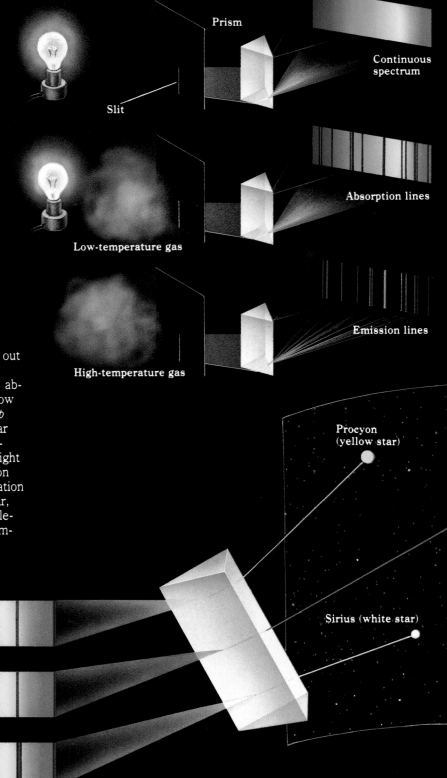

Prism

Slit

Continuous spectrum

Low-temperature gas

Absorption lines

High-temperature gas

Emission lines

Procyon (yellow star)

Sirius (white star)

Procyon: Type F5; Surface temperature 6,600° K

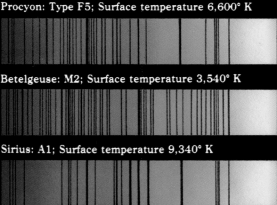

Betelgeuse: M2; Surface temperature 3,540° K

Sirius: A1; Surface temperature 9,340° K

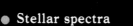

● Stellar spectra

By studying the spectra of stars, astronomers devised a system for classifying stars by their spectral type. The seven major types are O, B, A, F, G, K, and M. Hot blue or white stars are O, B, or A, cool red stars M. The Sun falls in-between, a G star. Astronomy students often remember spectral types from the phrase "Oh, Be A Fine Girl, Kiss Me."

Absorption lines in the spectrum of magnesium gas

Absorption lines in the spectrum of sodium gas

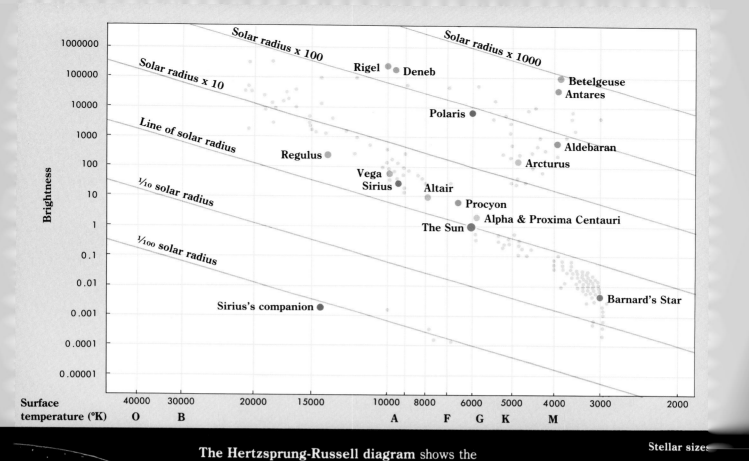

The Hertzsprung-Russell diagram
- Brightness (vertical axis): 0.00001, 0.0001, 0.001, 0.01, 0.1, 1, 10, 100, 1000, 10000, 100000, 1000000
- Surface temperature (°K): 40000, 30000, 20000, 15000, 10000, 8000, 6000, 5000, 4000, 3000, 2000
- Spectral types: O, B, A, F, G, K, M

Diagonal lines: Solar radius x 1000, Solar radius x 100, Solar radius x 10, Line of solar radius, 1/10 solar radius, 1/100 solar radius

Labeled stars: Rigel, Deneb, Betelgeuse, Antares, Polaris, Aldebaran, Regulus, Arcturus, Vega, Sirius, Altair, Procyon, Alpha & Proxima Centauri, The Sun, Barnard's Star, Sirius's companion

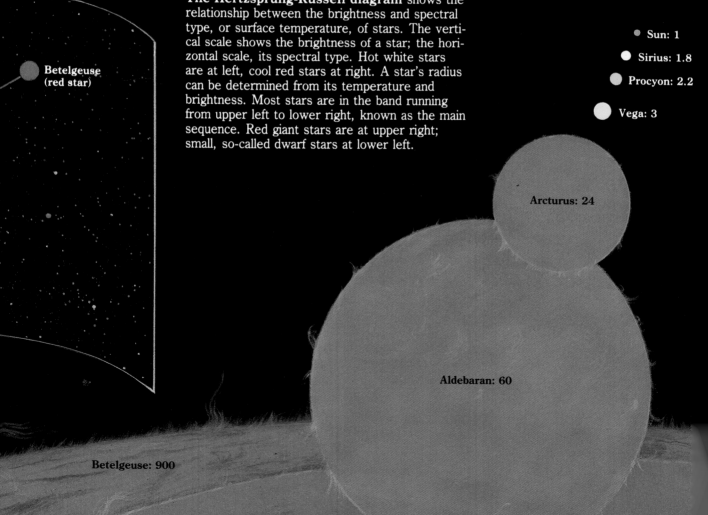

The Hertzsprung-Russell diagram shows the relationship between the brightness and spectral type, or surface temperature, of stars. The vertical scale shows the brightness of a star; the horizontal scale, its spectral type. Hot white stars are at left, cool red stars at right. A star's radius can be determined from its temperature and brightness. Most stars are in the band running from upper left to lower right, known as the main sequence. Red giant stars are at upper right; small, so-called dwarf stars at lower left.

Betelgeuse (red star)

Stellar sizes
- Sun: 1
- Sirius: 1.8
- Procyon: 2.2
- Vega: 3
- Arcturus: 24
- Aldebaran: 60
- Antares: 230
- Betelgeuse: 900

79

Why Are Some Stars Very Bright?

A star's brightness, as seen from Earth, depends on its temperature, its mass, and its distance from Earth. Astronomers classify stars according to their brightness, or magnitude. The lower the magnitude of a star, the brighter it is. A first-magnitude star is 2.5 times brighter than a second-magnitude star, which is 2.5 times brighter than a third-magnitude star. Stars dimmer than sixth magnitude cannot be seen with the naked eye. Since different stars are at different distances from Earth, this system of apparent magnitudes does not tell how bright a star really is. To determine the absolute magnitude, or intrinsic brightness, of a star, astronomers calculate how bright each star would be if it were at a distance of 32.6 light-years (about 200 trillion miles) away from Earth. Then they can tell whether a star appears to be bright because it is luminous or merely because it happens to be nearby.

Star

Earth

Absolute magnitude

Betelgeuse
−5.5

−3.8

−6.2   −6.2   −6.1

Earth

−6.2

Rigel
−6.6

● Apparent brightness

The apparent brightness of a star depends on how far away from Earth it is. Closer to Earth, the Sun would appear bigger and brighter. But seen from Pluto, the Sun appears small and is no brighter than Venus as seen from Earth. Brightness is inversely proportional to the square of distance: From twice as far away, the Sun would appear to be just one-fourth as bright.

● Apparent magnitude

There are two first-magnitude stars in Orion: Betelgeuse and Rigel. The apparent magnitude of Betelgeuse is 0.4, but it is 500 light-years away. If it were just 32.6 light-years away, its magnitude would be −5.5. Rigel is 700 light-years away; its apparent magnitude is 0.1, but its absolute magnitude is −6.6.

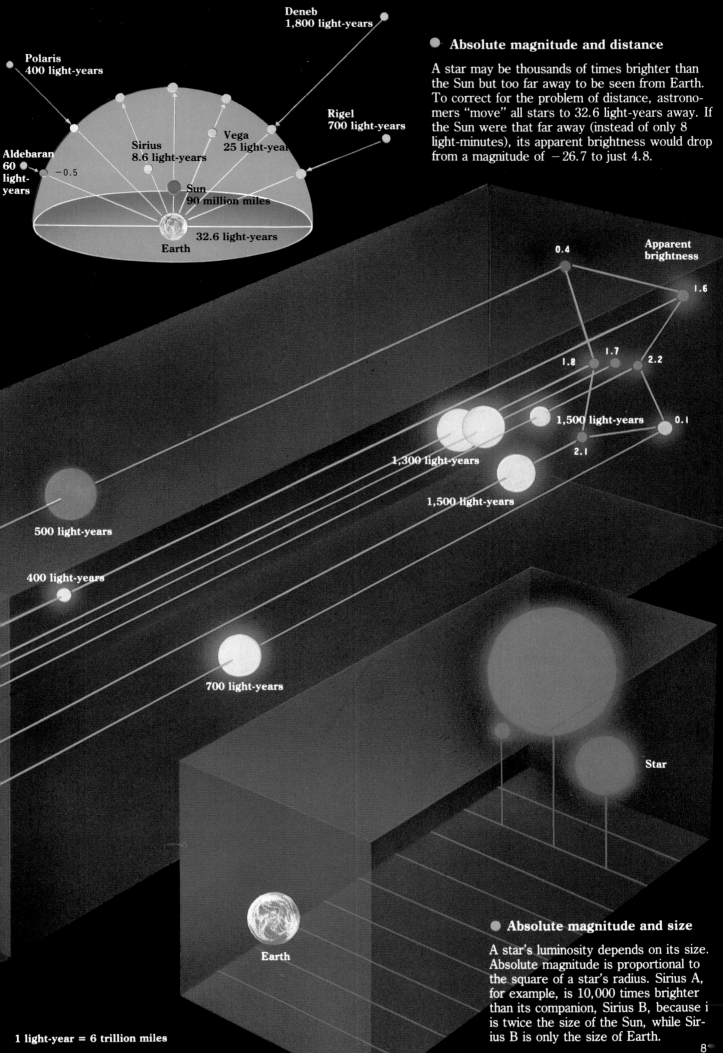

Polaris
400 light-years

Deneb
1,800 light-years

Aldebaran
60
light-
years

−0.5

Sirius
8.6 light-years

Vega
25 light-year

Rigel
700 light-years

Sun
90 million miles

32.6 light-years

Earth

Absolute magnitude and distance

A star may be thousands of times brighter than the Sun but too far away to be seen from Earth. To correct for the problem of distance, astronomers "move" all stars to 32.6 light-years away. If the Sun were that far away (instead of only 8 light-minutes), its apparent brightness would drop from a magnitude of − 26.7 to just 4.8.

0.4

Apparent
brightness

1.6

1.8   1.7   2.2

1,500 light-years   0.1

2.1

1,300 light-years

1,500 light-years

500 light-years

400 light-years

700 light-years

Earth

Star

Absolute magnitude and size

A star's luminosity depends on its size. Absolute magnitude is proportional to the square of a star's radius. Sirius A, for example, is 10,000 times brighter than its companion, Sirius B, because i is twice the size of the Sun, while Sirius B is only the size of Earth.

1 light-year = 6 trillion miles

8

What Are Variable Stars?

The Sun is a reliable source of light and energy, but not all stars are so constant. Some stars appear to flicker or pulsate, brightening and then dimming again over a period ranging from a few hours to several hundred days. There are two types of variable stars. Eclipsing variables, such as Algol, are binary star systems—stars that are circling each other—in which one star passes in front of the other, as seen from Earth. The amount of light from the binary varies according to the positions of the two stars, as seen from Earth. Pulsating variables are stars that expand and contract on a regular cycle. These are usually red giant stars, like Mira, whose nuclear reactions have become unstable with age. They brighten as they contract and dim as they expand.

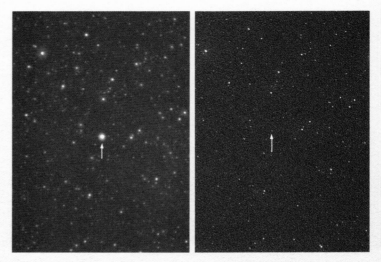

▲ **The red giant star Mira** pulsates from bright *(above left)* to dim *(above right)* as it goes through a regular 332-day cycle of contraction and expansion. Mira's magnitude varies from 2.0 to 10.1. The name Mira means "strange thing" in Latin. It was the first variable star to be discovered. German amateur astronomer David Fabricius spotted it in 1596.

● **Eclipsing Algol**

Algol is known as the winking devil *(below)*. First studied in 1669, Algol was later found to be two stars of different brightness. As the dimmer one passes in front of its companion, as seen from Earth, Algol "winks" and dims by about 1.3 magnitudes. The eclipses occur every 69 hours.

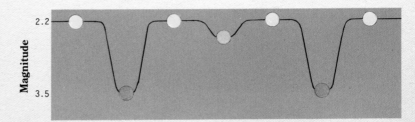

Algol's magnitude varies from 2.2 to 3.5.

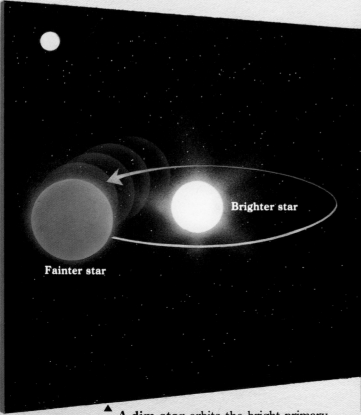

▲ **A dim star** orbits the bright primary.

▲ **Light from** the primary is eclipsed.

● Cepheid variables

The Cepheids are pulsating variable stars that expand and contract for periods between one and 50 days. Their brightness is related to the period of their variability; the absolute magnitude of a Cepheid can be determined from that period. With this data, astronomers can calculate the distance to any Cepheid.

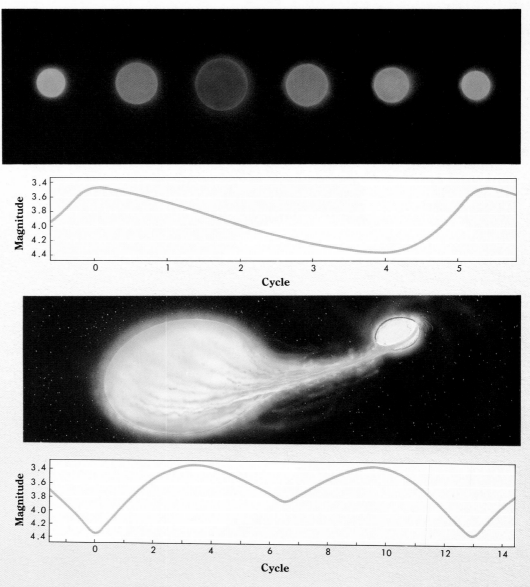

● Eclipsing Beta Lyrae

Beta Lyrae is an eclipsing variable that has long puzzled astronomers. Beta Lyrae's complex light curve seems to be the result of an exchange of mass between the two stars, orbiting very close to each other. The gravity of the more massive star pulls gases away from its companion. The disk of gases around the stars partially hides them, as seen from Earth.

▲ **The primary** emerges from the eclipse.

▲ **The primary** remains bright in this eclipse.

What Is a Supernova?

When an old, very massive star has consumed all its hydrogen fuel, it begins burning helium and carbon in its core. Without the hydrogen, there is not enough pressure in the core to counterbalance the inward pull caused by its great outer mass. Gravity causes the star to collapse, compressing the core. A violent explosion, called a supernova, follows and the star's remaining gases are blasted away into space. For a brief moment, the supernova outshines all the stars in the galaxy. Then it dims and only the dense core, composed entirely of neutrons, may remain. Or, an even denser black hole may form, with a gravitational force so great that not even light can escape from it.

Combustion of helium core

Combustion of carbon core

Start of gravitational collapse

Iron core

Type II supernova

A Type II supernova occurs when a star 10 or more times more massive than the Sun exhausts its nuclear fuel. These large stars, called red supergiants, can no longer generate enough nuclear energy to support their great mass. A gravitational collapse begins, compressing the core to a tremendous density and triggering a stream of particles that blasts away the star's gaseous shell. Nuclear fusion inside stars can create elements as heavy as iron. All elements heavier than iron are believed to be created in the forge of supernova explosions.

End of gravitational collapse

Shock waves

Neutron core

Shock waves

Neutron core

Heated gas

Supernova

84

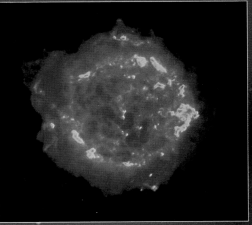

Legacies of supernovas. The Crab nebula *(left)* is an expanding shell of gas ejected by a supernova in 1054. A small, dense, rapidly rotating neutron star is at its center. Cassiopeia A *(above)* is the remnant of a supernova of 1572. A black hole is thought to lie at its center.

White dwarf

Red giant

● **Type I supernova**

A Type I supernova involves two stars in a binary system. The more massive star evolves into a red giant first, expanding close to its companion. The companion star tugs gases away from the larger star until the giant is stripped down to a white dwarf. The companion star in turn swells into a red giant and is stripped by its partner. Eventually all gaseous matter is dissipated and only two white dwarfs remain. They merge and explode. Unlike Type II supernovas, Type I supernovas are thought to leave nothing at all behind.

Supernova

What Is a Nebula?

A nebula (the Latin word for "cloud") is an interstellar cloud composed of hydrogen and helium and cosmic dust. Stars are born from the condensation of such clouds. When a star is near a nebula, its light is reflected from the cloud and the nebula appears to shine. The Pleiades star cluster is an example of such a reflection nebula. Ultraviolet radiation from a star within a nebula may excite the hydrogen atoms in the cloud and cause them to glow with a light of their own. The Orion nebula is such an emission nebula. Other nebulas may be dark because the dust in the cloud blocks out light from stars and gases behind them.

The North America nebula is an emission nebula with an odd but familiar shape.

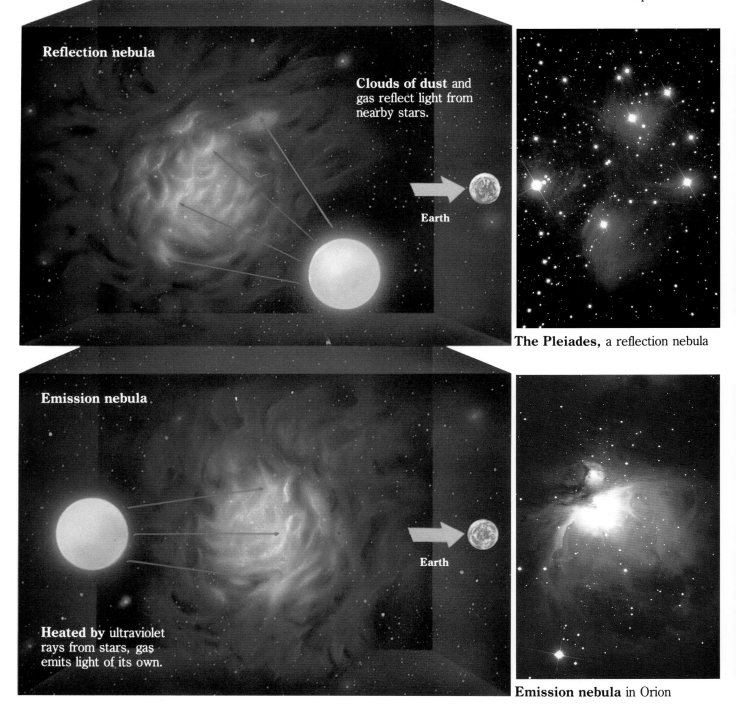

Reflection nebula

Clouds of dust and gas reflect light from nearby stars.

Earth

The Pleiades, a reflection nebula

Emission nebula

Earth

Heated by ultraviolet rays from stars, gas emits light of its own.

Emission nebula in Orion

A stellar nursery

Stars are born when a nebula fragments—sometimes because of shock waves from a nearby supernova—and collapses. Young, hot stars condense, usually in litters of several dozen, as in this nebula in the constellation Orion. Star formation occurs mainly in the arms of spiral galaxies, such as the Milky Way, where nebulas are common.

Planetary nebula

When an old star expands into a red giant, it may shed shells of gas, which glow from the star's ultraviolet radiation, appearing as a ring.

Earth

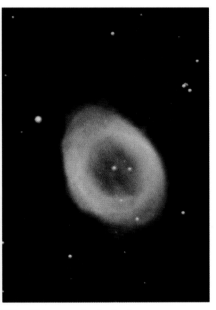

The Ring nebula in Lyra

Dark nebula

Earth

Dust may block light from stars, creating a dark patch in the sky.

The dark Horsehead nebula

How Did the Pleiades Cluster Form?

1 Starbirth begins when a shock wave fragments a nebula, which then collapses.

2 The collapsing cloud condenses into hot, young stars. Ultraviolet radiation that is emitted creates a region of high density.

Interstellar cloud

Newborn star

Denser portion of interstellar cloud

Shock waves

Newborn star

▼ **The Pleiades** are a favorite target for amateur astronomers. A small telescope or binoculars can reveal hundreds of these blue-white stars on late winter and early spring evenings.

One of the most beautiful sights in the night sky is the Pleiades, a star cluster in the constellation Taurus. The Pleiades are sometimes called "The Seven Sisters" because most people can see only seven of the stars with the naked eye. Yet the cluster actually contains some 3,000 stars. The Pleiades may be less than 100 million years old, which makes them some of the youngest stars we can see. New stars are probably still being born in the cluster, and the process, shown on these pages, will continue until the gas and dust in the nebula are used up. The bluish glow around the Pleiades is caused by the reflection of starlight from the nebula in which they are embedded.

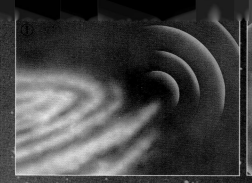

① ② ③

● Triggering starbirth

A nebula may be undisturbed for billions of years. In order for starbirth to begin, an external shock must cause the cloud to collapse. A shock may be provided by (1) a disturbance in the spiral arms of a galaxy, perhaps caused by a collision between galaxies; (2) a nearby supernova explosion; (3) ultraviolet radiation from a new star.

3 Gravity causes the cloud's dense region to contract more, providing materials for a new generation of stars.

4 The chain reaction of starbirth continues as the next generation of young stars produces more ultraviolet radiation, which in turn further increases the density of the remaining gas and dust in the cloud.

5 New stars continue to form until the gas and dust in the cloud are exhausted.

Shock waves

Denser portion of interstellar cloud

Denser portion of interstellar cloud

Do the Constellations Change?

Unlike the planets, which change their position in the sky from one night to the next, the stars never appear to move. In fact, however, the stars are constantly moving, some of them at great speed, but they are so far away that their motion cannot be detected with the unaided eye. In 1718, British astronomer Edmond Halley became the first to detect what is known as the proper motion of stars. This motion is so tiny that it can only be noticed over the course of many years. Today, for example, we know Polaris as the polestar because it is located above the North Pole. All the stars appear to revolve around Polaris, making it an important aid to navigation. But in ancient times, Polaris was elsewhere in the sky and could not be used as a guide star. Like Polaris, all the stars are slowly changing their position, and thousands of years from now, the familiar constellations will be completely unrecognizable.

The constellation Ursa Major, popularly known as the Big Dipper, is easy to identify. But each of the seven stars in the Dipper is at a different distance from Earth and each star moves in a different direction.

Changes in the Big Dipper

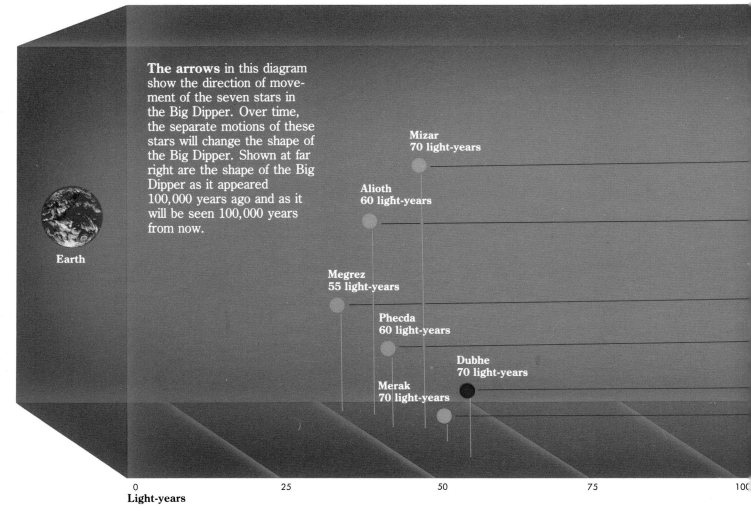

The arrows in this diagram show the direction of movement of the seven stars in the Big Dipper. Over time, the separate motions of these stars will change the shape of the Big Dipper. Shown at far right are the shape of the Big Dipper as it appeared 100,000 years ago and as it will be seen 100,000 years from now.

Earth

Mizar
70 light-years

Alioth
60 light-years

Megrez
55 light-years

Phecda
60 light-years

Dubhe
70 light-years

Merak
70 light-years

0   25   50   75   100
Light-years

Movement of stars

Determining the movement of stars can take years of patient observation. Alpha Centauri, for example, the closest star to the Sun, takes 506 years to move by as much as the apparent width of the full moon. Fortunately, astronomers can use another method to measure a star's motion—the Doppler effect. Waves of light (or sound) emitted by a moving object change their length according to whether the object is moving toward or away from the observer. Light waves from an approaching star are shortened—that is, they are shifted toward the blue end of the spectrum. Light from a receding star is shifted in the other direction—it is red-shifted. By measuring the amount of the shift, the speed of the star can be calculated.

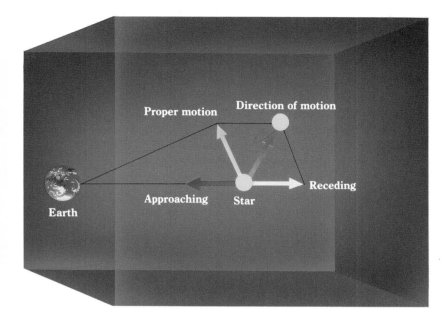

The Doppler effect

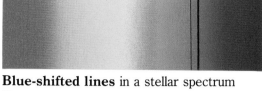

Blue-shifted lines in a stellar spectrum

Normal position of lines in a spectrum

Red-shifted lines in a stellar spectrum

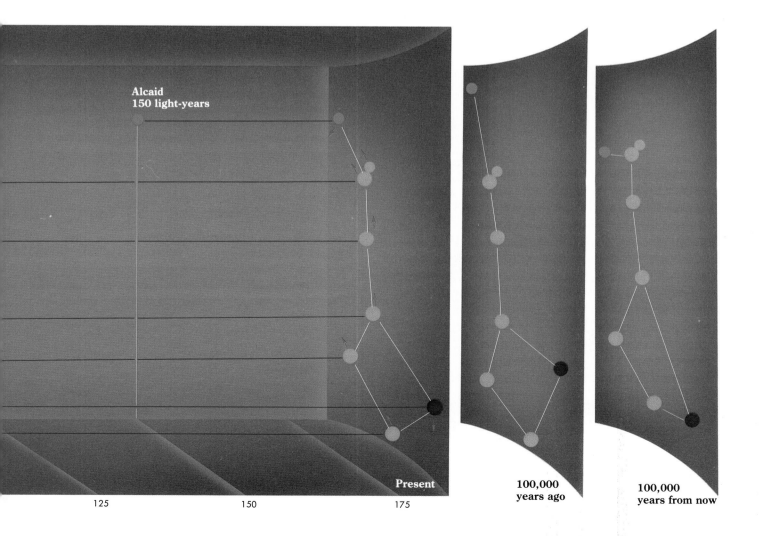

Alcaid
150 light-years

125   150   175   **Present**

100,000 years ago

100,000 years from now

How Do Stars Evolve?

For most of its lifetime, a typical star's properties fall in the main sequence of the Hertzsprung-Russell diagram *(page 79)*. In general, stars with a low mass tend to have longer lifetimes. A medium-size star like the Sun usually has a lifetime of about 10 billion years. Stars more massive than the Sun burn brighter but endure for a shorter time. When a Sun-size star exhausts its nuclear fuel, it expands for a brief time into a red giant, then shrinks and becomes a white dwarf. Massive stars swell up to become supergiants, before undergoing a supernova explosion.

Shock wave

Interstellar cloud

1 **Dense areas** in interstellar gas and dust clouds may be triggered into gravitational collapse by shock waves.

Shock wave

2 **The collapsing cloud** gradually forms into a flat, dense, pancake-shaped disk.

Dense section

3 **As the cloud shrinks,** the dense center begins to rotate rapidly, forming clumps.

4 **At the center** of a clump, density increases and a star begins to form. Pressure and temperature rise.

5 **The disk dissipates** as strong stellar winds blow outward from the protostar.

Protostar

6 **Pressure and** temperature in the protostar trigger nuclear reactions; the star begins to shine.

The birth of a star

Vast clouds of gas and dust in the arms of spiral galaxies provide the raw material for stars. As a cloud collapses, the density of matter at its center increases, causing temperature and pressure to rise to the point at which nuclear reactions can begin. The remaining cloud material may condense to form planets such as those in our solar system.

Stellar wind

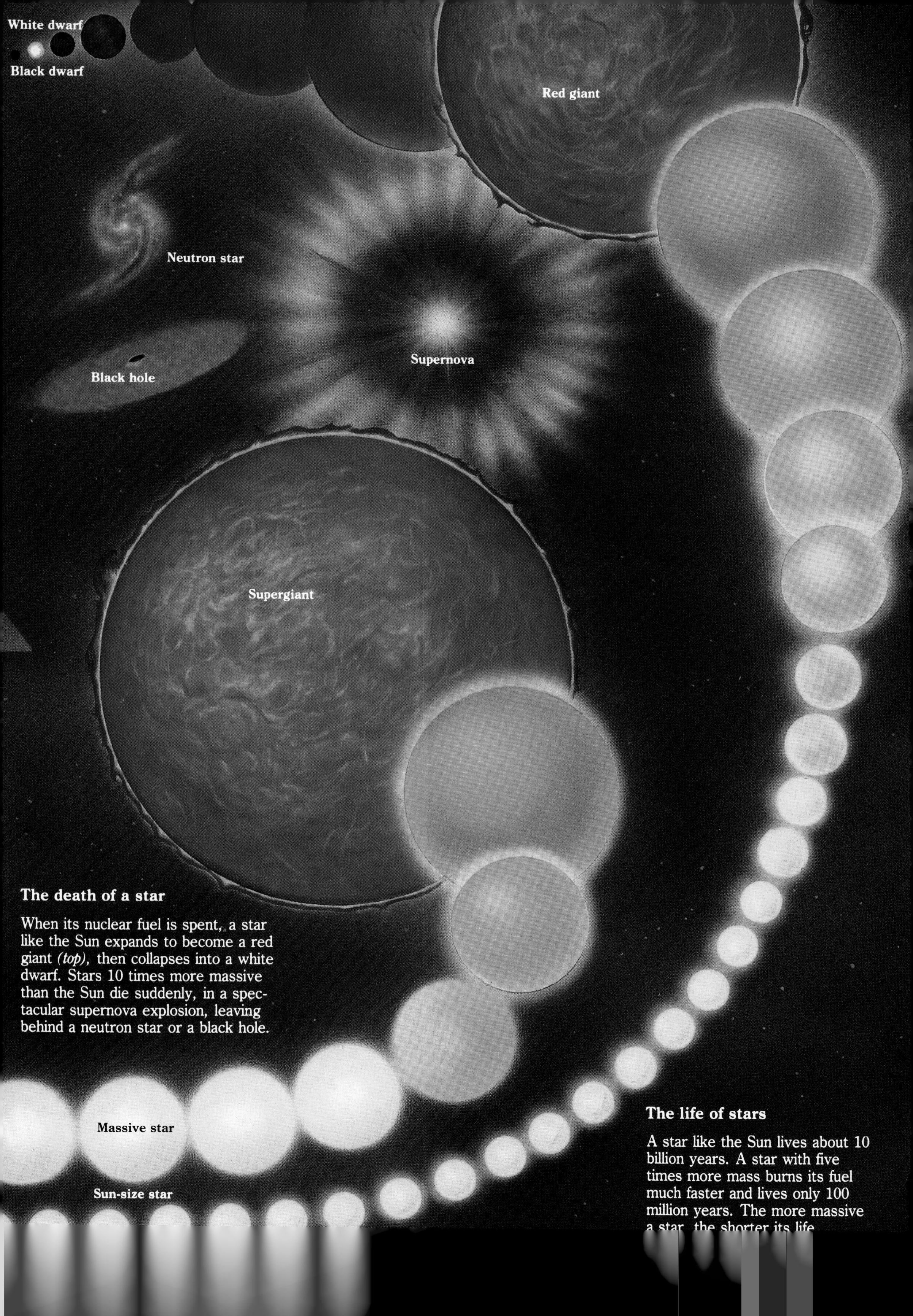

White dwarf

Black dwarf

Red giant

Neutron star

Black hole

Supernova

Supergiant

The death of a star

When its nuclear fuel is spent, a star like the Sun expands to become a red giant *(top)*, then collapses into a white dwarf. Stars 10 times more massive than the Sun die suddenly, in a spectacular supernova explosion, leaving behind a neutron star or a black hole.

Massive star

Sun-size star

The life of stars

A star like the Sun lives about 10 billion years. A star with five times more mass burns its fuel much faster and lives only 100 million years. The more massive a star, the shorter its life.

Many scientists believe that following a supernova explosion, a star's core collapses upon itself until it becomes only a point of infinite density. Its gravitational force becomes so great that nothing can escape from it, not even light—in effect, the black hole disappears from the universe. The very nature of a black hole makes it impossible to observe. Matter collects around the black hole, however, in what is known as an accretion disk; normal stars also become locked in an orbit around the black hole. Gradually, matter from the accretion disk is pulled into the black hole. As it disappears into the hole, the heated matter gives off bursts of x-rays, which can be detected. In order to find a black hole, astronomers look for x-ray signals and for normal stars that appear to be orbiting an empty place in space. They have found several black hole candidates, but so far the actual existence of a black hole has not been confirmed.

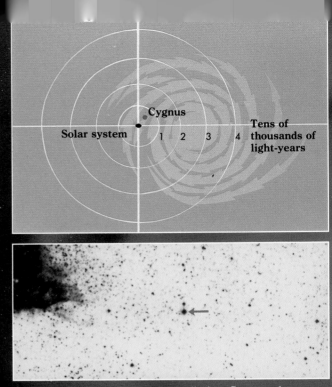

An x-ray source in the constellation Cygnus, known as Cygnus X-1 *(arrow)*, is a leading candidate for a black hole. Cygnus lies in the spiral arms of the Milky Way just 8,000 light-years from the Solar System.

Gas stream

Supergiant

A black hole scenario

The blue-white supergiant HDE226868, which is 20 times more massive than the Sun, forms a binary system with an unseen companion—possibly a black hole. Astronomers think that the powerful gravitational force of the black hole gradually strips gas from the giant star, and the gas forms an accretion disk around the black hole. At the inner edge of the accretion disk, the gas reaches extremely high temperatures before it is finally pulled into the hole. As it disappears, the gas emits powerful x-rays, which have been detected from Earth. The black hole remains undetectable.

Black hole

● Black hole signals

Black holes can only be detected indirectly. X-rays emitted from infalling matter and the odd motions of stars orbiting black holes are the most likely methods of detection. Black holes may also reveal their presence by their effect on light waves passing near them. Albert Einstein showed that light rays can be bent by the force of gravity. Light rays emitted from a source directly behind a black hole, as seen from Earth, would be warped around the black hole in what is known as a gravitational lens. Light distorted in this way appears to come from two separate but identical sources. Gravity waves, if they exist, would also indicate a black hole.

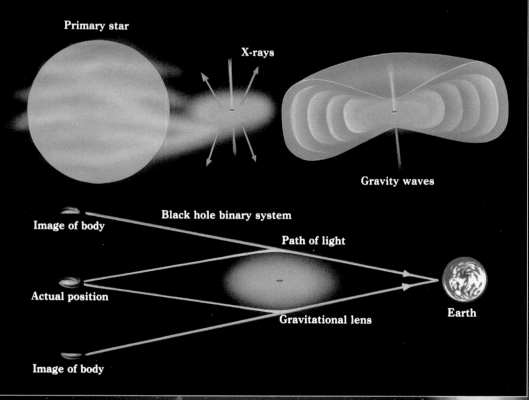

Primary star

X-rays

Gravity waves

Image of body

Black hole binary system

Path of light

Actual position

Gravitational lens

Earth

Image of body

After a supernova explosion, the remains of the dead star may fall inward and form either a black hole or a neutron star. The existence of black holes has not yet been verified, but many neutron stars have been detected. Neutrons are heavy particles in the center of atoms. In a neutron star, other particles, such as protons and electrons, have been stripped away, leaving only a small sphere of closely packed neutrons. A neutron star may be just 6 miles in diameter, yet have more mass than the Sun. A spoonful of neutron star matter would weigh a billion tons or more. Neutron stars spin very rapidly, radiating energy as they rotate. That energy may be detected as radio waves or as x-rays.

▲ **The Crab nebula** is a shell of gas left from a supernova of the year 1054. At its center, a pulsar rotates 30 times a second.

■ Bursts of energy

A neutron star emits radiation along the axis of its magnetic field. Because the magnetic axis is not perfectly lined up with the axis of rotation, the emissions sweep across the sky like a searchlight. When the emissions sweep by Earth once or twice in each rotation, they seem to pulse on and off, and the stars are called pulsars. Neutron stars are often detected in binary systems as x-ray pulsars, in which matter from the companion star is drawn toward the neutron star. As gas falls on the neutron star's surface, it emits bursts of x-rays.

Gas flow

Primary star

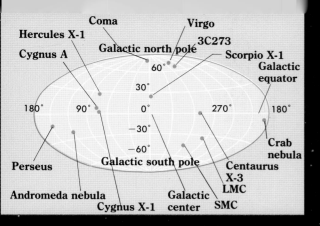

Coma
Hercules X-1   Virgo
Cygnus A   3C273
    Galactic north pole
              60°   Scorpio X-1
                              Galactic
        30°   equator
180°   90°   0°   270°   180°
              −30°
              −60°
Perseus   Galactic south pole
                         Centaurus
                         X-3
                         LMC
Andromeda nebula   Galactic
         Cygnus X-1   center   SMC
                              Crab
                              nebula

Astronomers have found hundreds of x-ray sources *(left)*. A few may be neutron stars or black holes and one a massive black hole at the center of the Milky Way. X-rays from space cannot be detected from Earth, but orbiting observatories will aid the search.

● Pulsing signals

As it rotates, the magnetic axis of a neutron star sweeps through the sky like a searchlight. Neutron star emissions can only be detected when the searchlight points at Earth.

To Earth

Lines of magnetic force

X-rays

Axis of rotation

Magnetic pole

Neutron star

Outer core
Inner core
Sea of neutron superfluid
Exotic particles

X-rays

6
Galaxies and the Universe

The universe contains hundreds of billions of galaxies: vast celestial bodies of light cradling countless stars, gas, and cosmic dust. Our home galaxy, the Milky Way, holds more than 100 billion stars, including our sun and its solar system. Like many of the galaxies in the universe, the Milky Way is a spiral-shaped disk with a bulge at the center. Other galaxies are elliptical—similar to flattened balls—or irregular, with random groupings of stars.

Most galaxies revolve around a brilliantly lit bulging center, densely packed with millions of stars. Each core contains a highly charged energy source, believed to be fueled by a black hole, a mysterious object of such density that nothing, not even light, can escape from its boundaries.

Even more puzzling than the source of a galaxy's power is the curious fact that all galaxies appear to be moving away from one another in every direction. This observation has led most astronomers to conclude that the universe is expanding and that it was set into motion some 15 billion years ago by a cataclysmic explosion known as the Big Bang. Scientists do not know for sure what the ultimate fate of our universe will be. Some think it will expand indefinitely, while others believe that it will eventually contract and collapse into one supercharged, superdense mass. Whatever the answer, astronomers will continue to probe the depths of the universe, solving its mysteries one step at a time.

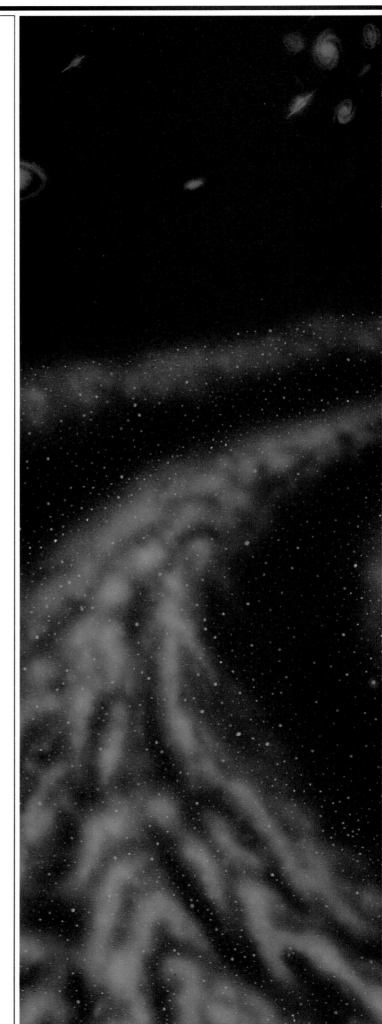

Billions of stars spiral around a central bulge in a galaxy similar to our own Milky Way.

The Milky Way, seen as a spectacular band of stars across the night sky, is the visible portion of a spiraling, disk-shaped galaxy. So vast is our home galaxy, it would take a ray of light 100,000 years to cross its width. The Sun, once thought to be at the center of the Milky Way, actually lies about two-thirds out from the core in the spiral arms of the Galaxy. More than a billion stars join the Sun in its journey around the center; most lie in the spiral arms of the disk, but some are widely scattered, encircling the Galaxy like a halo of faint light.

The Milky Way, near Sagittarius, lights up the sky.

■ **The Galaxy** as seen from Earth

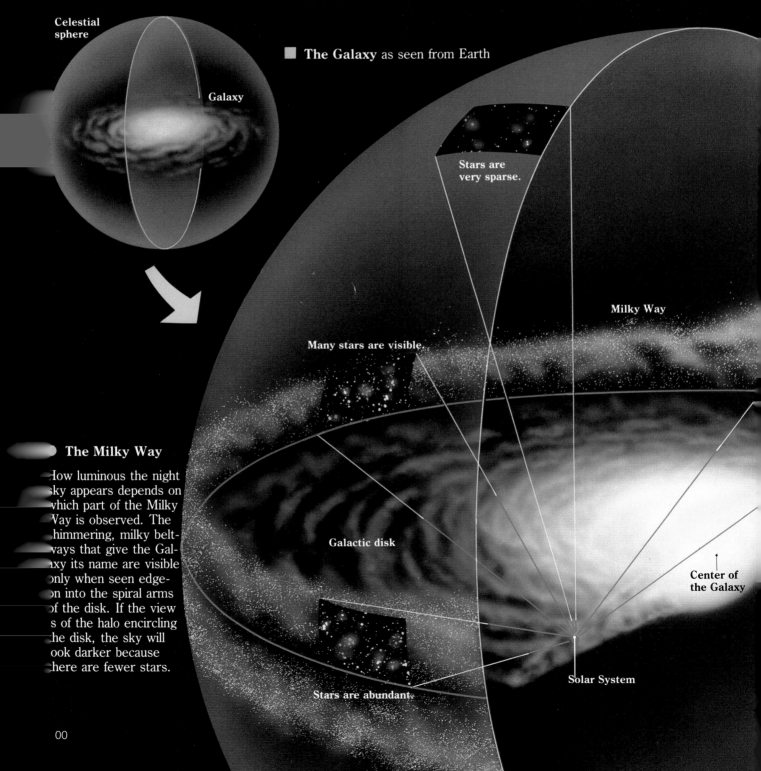

Celestial sphere

Galaxy

Stars are very sparse.

Milky Way

Many stars are visible.

Galactic disk

Center of the Galaxy

Solar System

Stars are abundant.

The Milky Way

How luminous the night sky appears depends on which part of the Milky Way is observed. The shimmering, milky belt-ways that give the Galaxy its name are visible only when seen edge-on into the spiral arms of the disk. If the view is of the halo encircling the disk, the sky will look darker because there are fewer stars.

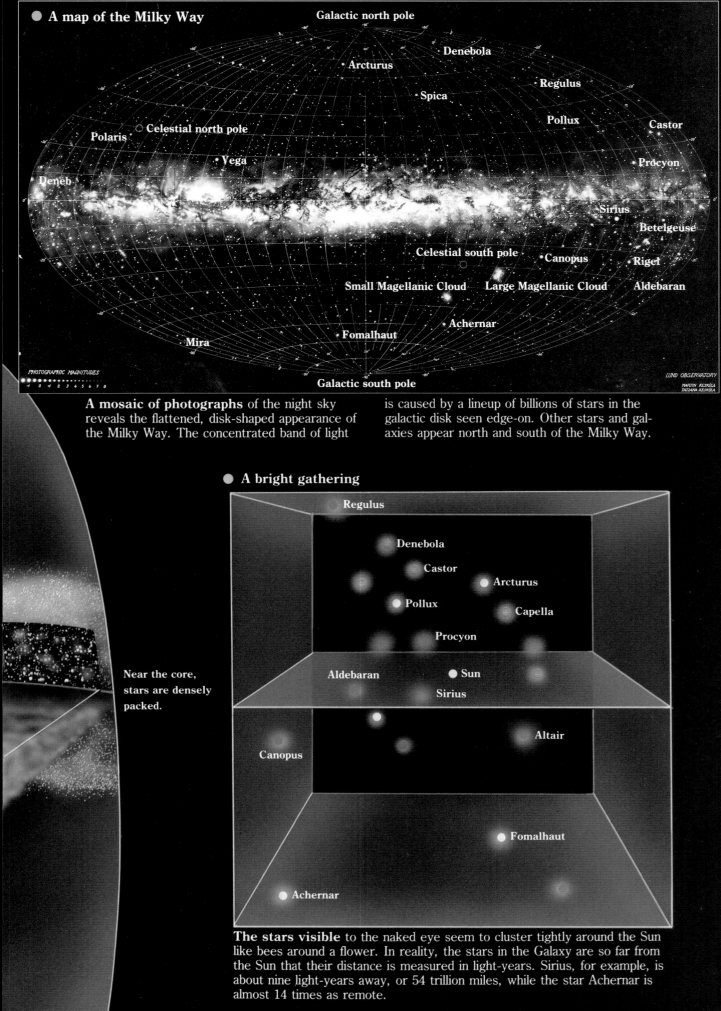

A map of the Milky Way

Galactic north pole

Denebola

Arcturus

Regulus

Spica

Pollux

Castor

Celestial north pole

Procyon

Polaris

Vega

Deneb

Sirius

Betelgeuse

Celestial south pole

Canopus

Rigel

Small Magellanic Cloud

Large Magellanic Cloud

Aldebaran

Achernar

Fomalhaut

Mira

PHOTOGRAPHIC MAGNITUDES

LUND OBSERVATORY
MARTIN KESKÜLA
TATIANA KESKÜLA

Galactic south pole

A mosaic of photographs of the night sky reveals the flattened, disk-shaped appearance of the Milky Way. The concentrated band of light is caused by a lineup of billions of stars in the galactic disk seen edge-on. Other stars and galaxies appear north and south of the Milky Way.

A bright gathering

Regulus

Denebola

Castor

Arcturus

Pollux

Capella

Procyon

Near the core, stars are densely packed.

Aldebaran

Sun

Sirius

Altair

Canopus

Fomalhaut

Achernar

The stars visible to the naked eye seem to cluster tightly around the Sun like bees around a flower. In reality, the stars in the Galaxy are so far from the Sun that their distance is measured in light-years. Sirius, for example, is about nine light-years away, or 54 trillion miles, while the star Achernar is almost 14 times as remote.

What Is the Structure of the Galaxy?

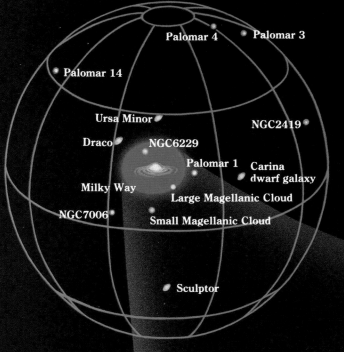

Palomar 4   Palomar 3

Palomar 14

Ursa Minor   NGC2419

Draco   NGC6229

Palomar 1   Carina
                    dwarf galaxy

Milky Way
                    Large Magellanic Cloud

NGC7006   Small Magellanic Cloud

Sculptor

The Milky Way galaxy spins through the universe like a colossal pinwheel thrown from the hands of a cosmic giant. At its center lies a thick bulge made up of a billion densely packed old stars. Emanating from this bulge are two arm-like structures holding younger stars, dust, and gas. These arms wind about the center as it turns, giving our galaxy its spiral appearance. Although the Milky Way counts among the large galaxies in the universe, it is only a minute speck among billions of galaxies varying greatly in size and shape.

● **The Galaxy's neighborhood**

Nestled inside a globe-shaped neighborhood of galaxies, the Milky Way serves as the focus for other galaxies, called the Local Group. More than 30 such galaxies gather here, held together by mutual gravitational attraction.

Halo

Galactic disk

Bulge

Solar System

● **Galactic disk and halo**

Rotating inside a halo of hot gas and orbiting stars, the Milky Way is dissected here to reveal the structure of its disk. Radiating from the thick center is the yellow glow of aging stars; as the disk thins, it shines with the blue light of newborn stars. The halo—about 400,000 light-years wide—may be the remnant gas from which our galaxy was made.

Galaxies come in four basic shapes: spiral, barred spiral, elliptical, and irregular. Spirals are most prominent, though ellipticals are more plentiful. Spirals consist of a bright core with rotating arms; a barred spiral's arms emerge from a bar that extends beyond the core. Ellipticals' cores fade almost to the edges of the galaxy. Irregular galaxies, the least common, do not rotate about a central core.

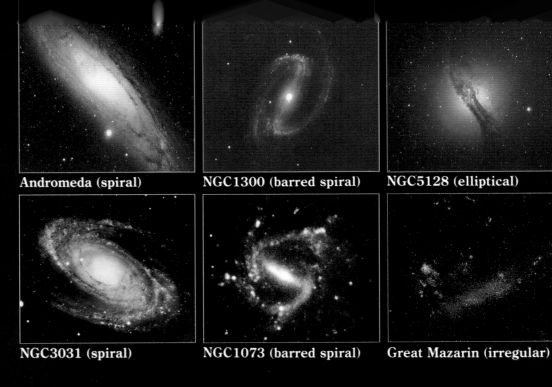

Andromeda (spiral)

NGC1300 (barred spiral)

NGC5128 (elliptical)

NGC3031 (spiral)

NGC1073 (barred spiral)

Great Mazarin (irregular)

● Projection of the Galaxy

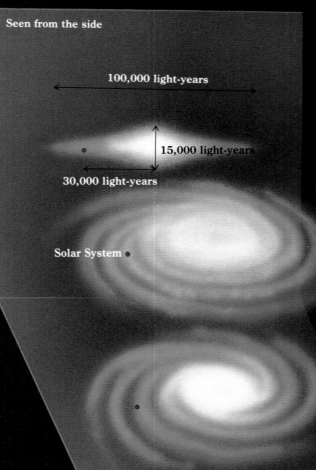

Seen from the side

100,000 light-years

15,000 light-years

30,000 light-years

Plane of the galactic disk

Solar System

Seen from above

When viewed from the side, the Milky Way galaxy looks like two cymbals clapped together *(top)*. Its diameter is 100,000 light-years across and 15,000 light-years thick at the core. The arms of the Galaxy can be seen coiling around the central bulge *(center and bottom)*. The Sun, the Earth, and the other planets spin 30,000 light-years from the center and are situated in the Orion arm of the spiral. It takes the Sun over 250 million years to finish one full revolution around the center.

What Is the Galaxy's Center Like?

Galaxy

Billions of stars blaze from the Milky Way's center and revolve more rapidly than any other part of the Galaxy. For years, astronomers have been unable to see into the inner regions of the core because it is hidden by stars and clouds of dust and gas. Now, with infrared and radio telescopes, they are beginning to get a picture of how this colossal engine powers the Galaxy. The most surprising discovery is a magnetic whirlpool-like structure at the heart of the Galaxy. From here erupts a gas jet that shoots some 12,000 light-years into space. Astronomers think that the jet is fueled by a supermassive black hole with the mass of a large star but with the energy output of 100 billion suns.

Bulge

Jet

Low-density gas

Jet

The bulge

Normally shielded from view by a dense halo of old stars, the interior of the Galaxy's bulge reveals spiral arms of low-density gas. Located inside the bulge about 10,000 light-years from the core, the arms whip around the center at about 80 miles per second, expanding and flattening out into a disk.

Core

Core disk

Core disk

About 1,000 light-years from the core's center lies a ring of high-density gas, containing dust and molecules and, possibly, young stars. A jet of gas spouts for thousands of light-years through the center of the disk. These jets are shaped by a powerful magnetic field perpendicular to the disk.

Galactic center radio source

A radio map from the Nobeyama Radio Observatory in Japan shows a close-up of the Galaxy's center. Concentric circles indicate levels of intensity of a source of furious heat and energy—perhaps a black hole. The black hole's gravity is causing neighboring stars and matter to fall into the black hole, heating the matter to extremely high temperatures and generating explosive radiation. The snakelike projection to the left of the core appears to be a jet of hot gas. Astronomers are still not certain of its cause.

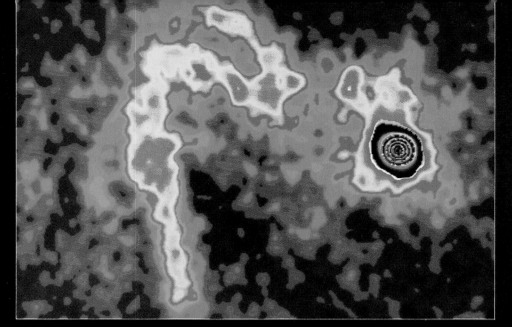

The heart of the Galaxy

Encircled by two cold rings of gas and a very hot inner ring, the Galaxy's core appears as a rotating disk about three light-years in diameter. Scientists concluded that only a supermassive black hole five million times the Sun's mass could produce the prodigious amounts of energy emanating from this core. As gravity pulls in surrounding matter, friction from in-falling particles generates soaring temperatures and radiation.

Core

Spiral arms

Gas disk

Why Is the Milky Way a Spiral?

1

■ **The Milky Way's spiral arms**

2

In this demonstration of the creation of a spiral pattern, stars line up along an imaginary starting gate on either side of the center of the Galaxy, much like runners about to begin a race around a track.

3

Each star moves clockwise around the center at its own rate. The innermost stars complete an orbit around the center about once every 20 million years, while the stars on the outer edge may take 10 times as long to make the trip.

The spiraling arms of stars, gas, and dust that revolve around the Galaxy's core prove to be one of the more mysterious puzzles in the universe. The exact origin of the spiral is not known, nor are astronomers absolutely certain how the disk keeps its spiral shape. Like a string tied around a spinning top, the arms should have coiled tightly around the Galaxy's center by now. Astronomers believe that the spiral stays in place because of waves that move through the stars and gas like ripples in a pond. They think that these waves were set into motion by powerful gravitational disturbances that took place in the Galaxy's formation billions of years ago. Moving more slowly than the stars and gas that populate the Galaxy's spiral highways, the waves cause enormous tie-ups of matter that result in the creation of new stars. Many of these new stars are so huge that they eventually explode, sending more shock waves through the system. The combination of the rippling wave pattern and the starbirths may help to maintain the spiral shape and keep it stocked with new material.

▼ **Swirling clouds of stars,** gas, and dust dance around the small, bright nucleus of spiral galaxy M51, some 21 million light-years from Earth.

Direction of rotation of spiral arms

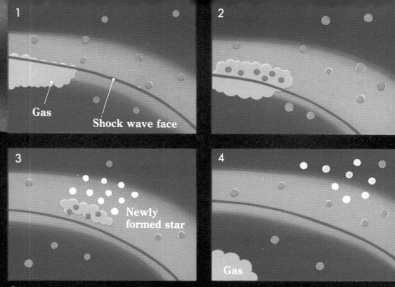

Center

Spiral arms

Direction of rotation of gas

Shock wave face

1

Gas

Shock wave face

2

3

Newly formed star

4

Gas

One theory for the Galaxy's constant spiral shape is explained above in an enlarged view of a spiral arm. The strong gravitational pull of a spiral arm *(pink)* attracts a cloud of low density gas *(green)* into its field. As the cloud tries to push through the densely packed stars and gas, it gets stalled, much like a car caught in a traffic jam. Pressure builds in the cloud until it finally "bursts," spewing forth new bright stars. Because these stars are plentiful in number and highly energetic, they are able to push their way through the crowd. Other stars explode in the process, while some remain in the arm, continuing to orbit around the Galaxy. This pattern of events sends shock waves through the system, which may keep the spiral arms pushed apart, even as their spinning presses them toward the center.

4

By the time the innermost stars have wound around the center 1½ times, the outer stars are trailing behind at ever greater distances.

The spiral pattern becomes more obvious as the innermost stars outpace their far-flung neighbors. Surprisingly, the spiral arms never wind up completely, an effect that astronomers believe is due to some unique characteristics of the disk itself *(above)*.

How Was the Universe Formed?

The universe probably began some 15 billion years ago with the Big Bang, a fiery explosion from a point of infinite density that propelled time, space, energy, and matter into being. Seconds after the explosion, the universe was a seething soup of radiation and exotic particles. As the universe expanded, it grew cooler and less dense. After hundreds of thousands of years, electrons, protons, and neutrons joined to form hydrogen and helium atoms. One billion years after the Big Bang, gravity pulled these gases into enormous clouds, known as protogalaxies. A billion years later, the protogalaxies spawned the first stars. Today, the universe looks like a vast bubble, with clusters of galaxies forming walls around great voids.

Big Bang

Rapid expansion

1 In the very early fractions of time after the Big Bang *(left)*, the universe grew rapidly, inflating from the size of a pin to about 2,000 times the size of the Sun.

2 Before the universe was one second old *(above)*, it was a hot, swirling mass of the most elementary particles. It was also as dense as iron, so opaque that no light could shine through.

Birth of atoms

Electron

Proton

Neutron

Hydrogen atom

Helium atom

3 After the first 500,000 years *(above)*, the universe gradually cooled to 3,000° K. The elementary particles fused, forming the lifeblood of the universe: hydrogen and helium gas. The faint cosmic glow of 3° K microwave radiation that is visible today throughout the universe is thought to be the remnant of the Big Bang.

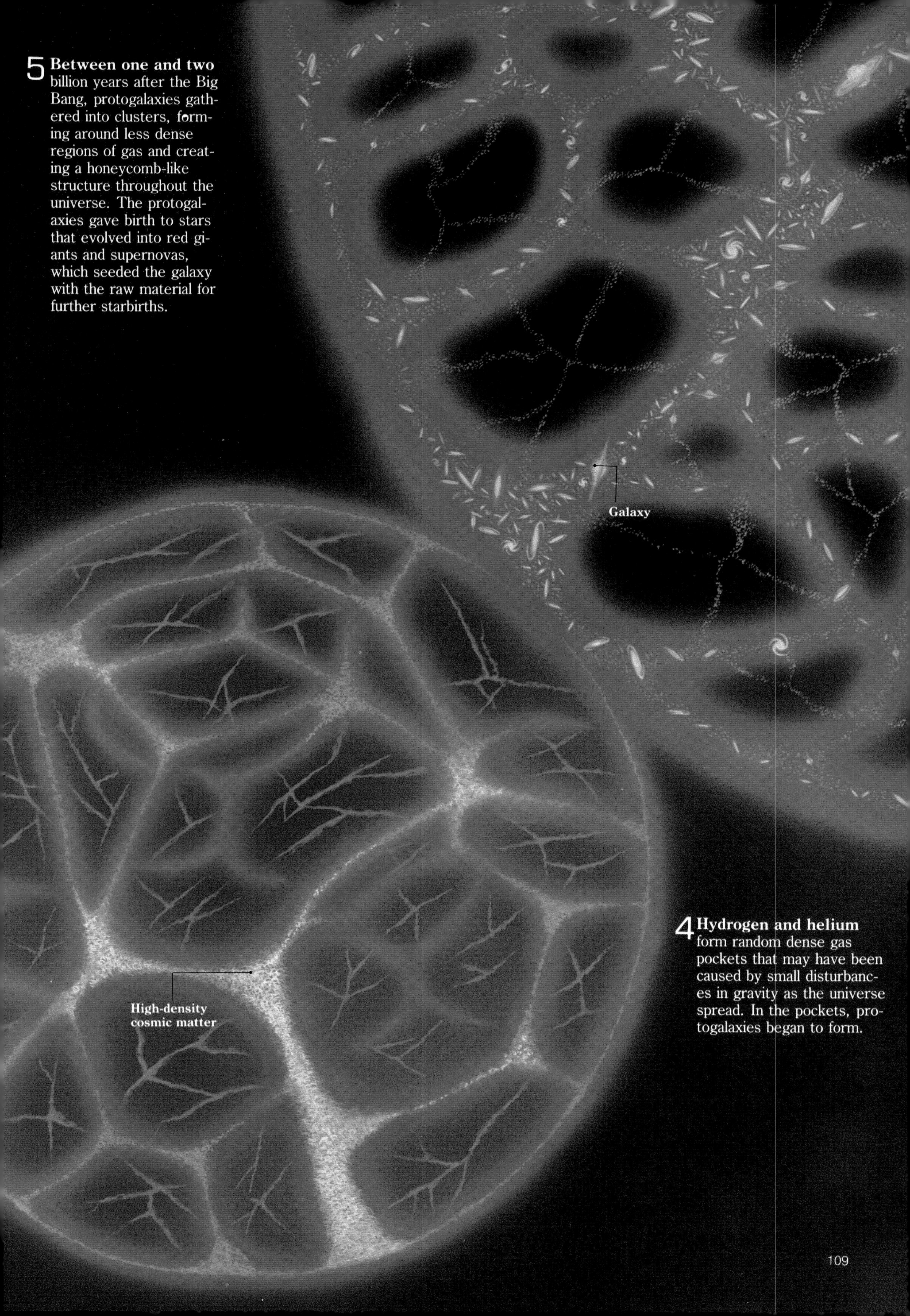

5 Between one and two billion years after the Big Bang, protogalaxies gathered into clusters, forming around less dense regions of gas and creating a honeycomb-like structure throughout the universe. The protogalaxies gave birth to stars that evolved into red giants and supernovas, which seeded the galaxy with the raw material for further starbirths.

Galaxy

4 Hydrogen and helium form random dense gas pockets that may have been caused by small disturbances in gravity as the universe spread. In the pockets, protogalaxies began to form.

High-density
cosmic matter

What Is the Structure of the Universe?

● Cluster upon cluster

Superclusters, massive gatherings of galaxy clusters held together by gravity, form bubblelike walls. Clusters cover areas 30 million to 40 million light-years across; superclusters are 10 times larger.

Clusters of superclusters

Supercluster (enlarged view)

● The Local Supercluster

A small portion of the Local Supercluster that contains our Local Group is shown in the illustration below. It stretches about 150 million light-years through space.

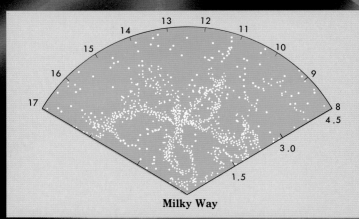

13 12 11
14
15 10
16 9
17 8
4.5
3.0
1.5
Milky Way

In this fan-shaped slice of the universe, as seen from Earth, superclusters settle like suds around empty bubbles of space. The largest concentration at the center marks the Virgo cluster.

M33

Astronomers estimate there could be up to 100 billion galaxies in the universe, and nearly all of them seem to gather into recognizable groups, or clusters. Gravity binds the galaxies together. The Milky Way is part of a neighborhood cluster of some 30 galaxies known as the Local Group, spread over a region 30 million light-years across. Some galaxy clusters are small; others contain thousands of members, stretching across millions upon millions of light-years. These galaxy clusters in turn collect in an even larger gathering known as a supercluster. Our Local Group is part of the Local Supercluster, which holds more than 100 clusters. Both clusters and superclusters settle in dense pathways around black voids of space, giving the universe a bubblelike appearance. Astronomers suspect there may also be clusters of superclusters.

The Milky Way galaxy

Although the Milky Way galaxy is the second largest member of the Local Group, it accounts for only a small portion of the total volume.

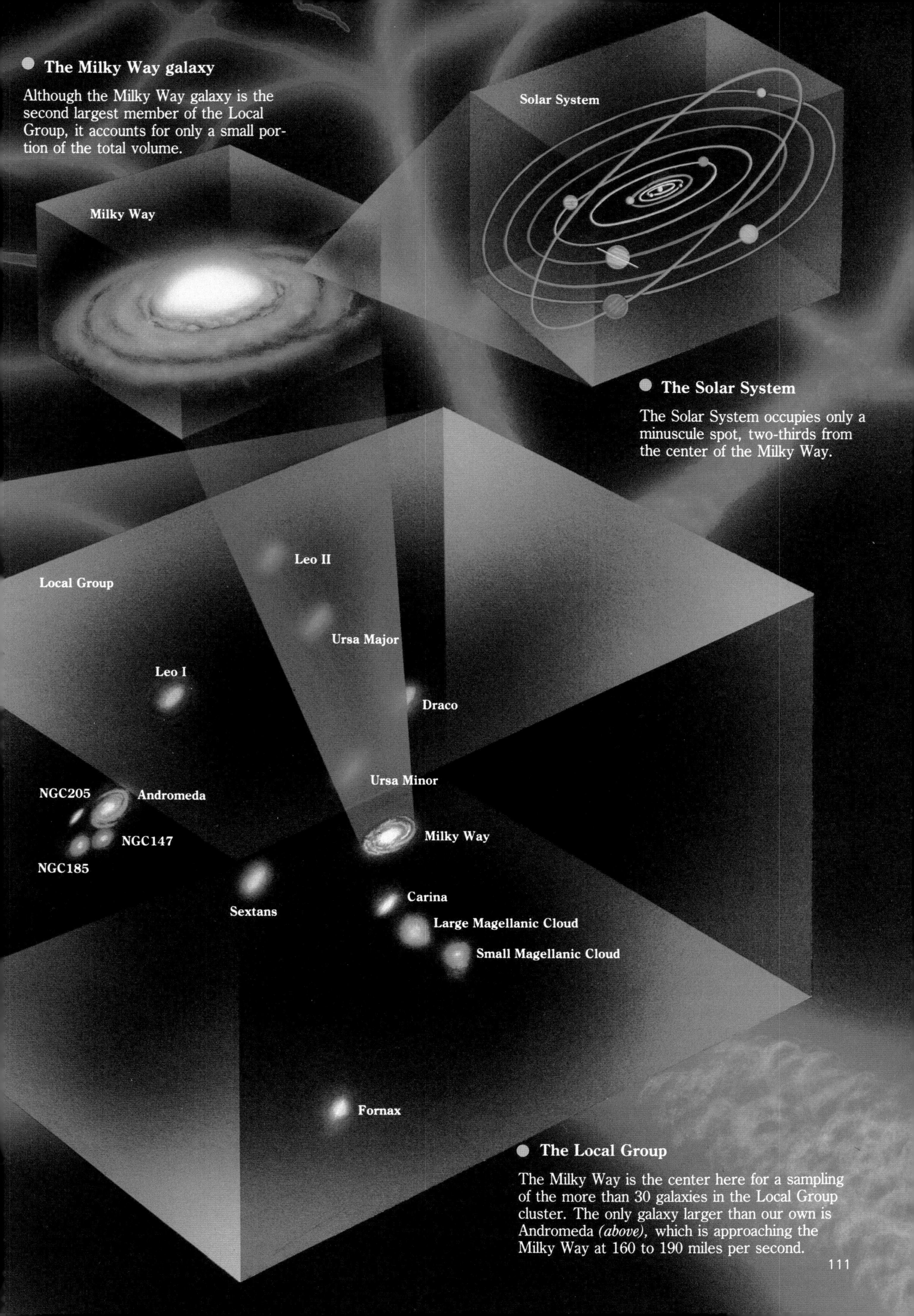

Milky Way

Solar System

The Solar System

The Solar System occupies only a minuscule spot, two-thirds from the center of the Milky Way.

Leo II

Local Group

Ursa Major

Leo I

Draco

Ursa Minor

NGC205 Andromeda

NGC147

Milky Way

NGC185

Carina

Sextans

Large Magellanic Cloud

Small Magellanic Cloud

Fornax

The Local Group

The Milky Way is the center here for a sampling of the more than 30 galaxies in the Local Group cluster. The only galaxy larger than our own is Andromeda *(above)*, which is approaching the Milky Way at 160 to 190 miles per second.

111

What Are Quasars?

In the early 1960s, astronomers detected strong radio signals coming from faint, starlike objects. Astronomers named them quasars, for quasi-stellar radio sources. The mysterious sources' spectra showed emission lines that were shifted far to the red, which meant that they were located far from Earth and were moving away at phenomenal speeds. Furthermore, quasars appeared to be smaller than galaxies. Astronomers were mystified by how objects of this size could still put out such intense radiation. They concluded that quasars possessed an incomprehensible brightness—some as much as a trillion times brighter than the Sun. One theory suggests giant black holes as the cause of the quasars' brightness and proposes that quasars are the extremely luminous centers of infant galaxies. Quasars only appear faint because they are so distant. The nearest quasars are three billion light-years from Earth, while the most remote ones may be six times as far. Astronomers have yet to discover objects farther away or older than quasars—some date back to a time when the universe was only two billion years old. Quasars, then, are gateways to the past, giving scientists a tantalizing look at the conditions immediately following the Big Bang.

Nearby galaxies

Milky Way stars

Earth

0.0

10^3

10^2

Distance (in light-years)
Speed of recession
(speed of light = 1)

Ionized hydrogen
and helium

Cosmic background
radiation

Atomic hydrogen
and helium

Protogalaxies

Primeval galaxies

Quasars

Galaxies too faint
to be seen

Remote galaxies

0.99999

0.9999

0.999

1.64×10¹⁰

0.99

1.5×10¹⁰

0.9

0.7

0.5

10¹⁰

0.1

10⁹

0.01

10⁸

● A puzzling radiance

Spouting from the upper right of quasar 3C273 is
a faint gas jet, which scientists believe is the result of a gigantic black hole at its center. The
black hole may also account for the quasar's extreme brightness, giving off as much energy in
one second as the Sun emits in 300,000 years.

● Cosmic evolution

To look into space from Earth is to look back in time, as
this cone-shaped view of the universe reveals. A nearby
galaxy 10 million light-years away is seen as it was 10
million years ago because its light took that long to
reach us. The region at the far edge of the cone *(above,
far right)* depicts the early years after the Big Bang,
when the universe glowed with cosmic background radiation. This was followed by a rapid cooling in which matter solidified to form protogalaxies. The first quasars
discovered were closer in, about three billion light-years
away. Astronomers think these younger quasars are
galaxies in the making. Closer to the present, quasars
fade, replaced by the more abundant "normal" galaxies.

Is the Universe Expanding?

Astronomers once thought that the universe was infinitely large but that it never changed its shape or size. Then, in the late 1920s, American astronomer Edwin P. Hubble made a startling discovery after plotting the distances between galaxies and comparing them to their speeds of recession: The more distant a galaxy was from our own, the faster it moved away.

Hubble's law, as it came to be called, led astronomers to one inescapable conclusion: If galaxies were rushing away from each other in all directions, then the universe was expanding. Whether that will continue is still a mystery.

Galaxy

Hubble's law

The diagram illustrates the principle of Hubble's law: The farther a galaxy cluster is from any other cluster along the line, the faster it moves away.

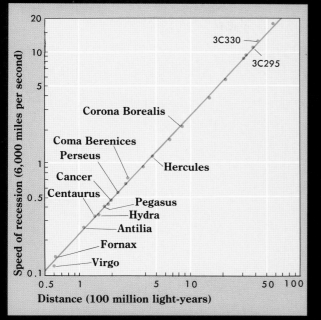

Speed of recession (6,000 miles per second)

3C330
3C295

Corona Borealis

Coma Berenices
Perseus
Cancer
Centaurus
Hercules
Pegasus
Hydra
Antilia
Fornax
Virgo

Distance (100 million light-years)

Universal expansion

Using a single galaxy as a starting point *(left)*, all other galaxies are moving away from it at speeds relative to their distance. Quasars, for example, are the most remote objects in the universe. As shown below, their absorption lines are shifted toward the red end of the spectrum *(top)*, which means that they are receding at faster speeds than objects closer in *(middle and bottom)*. Even if another galaxy were to be used as a point of origin, the relationship between speed and distance would remain the same. This constant suggests that the universe is expanding in all directions.

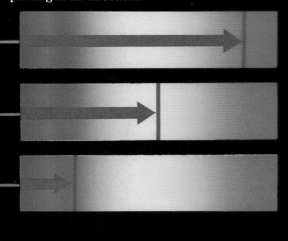

Open or closed universe?

One of two fates awaits the universe. Below a critical density, equal to three hydrogen atoms per 35 cubic feet, the universe cannot muster enough gravity to hold together and will expand forever *(below, right)*. With more than critical density, gravity will cause the universe to collapse into the Big Crunch.

Closed universe   **Open universe**

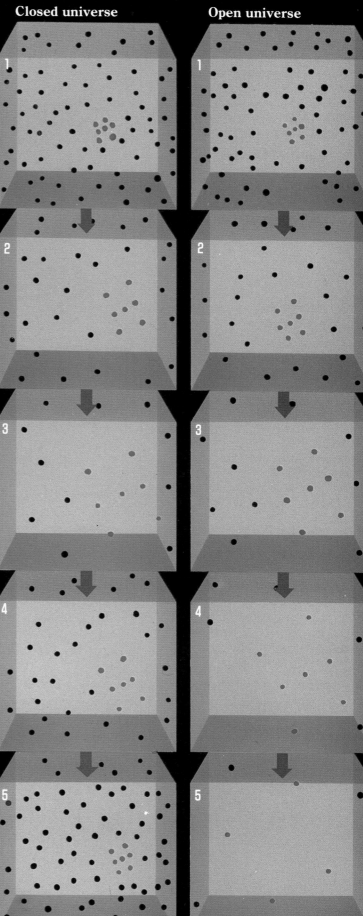

7
Watching the Skies

Before there were telescopes, there was the human eye. With it, early astronomers built the foundations of their science. They named the visible stars and the patterns they made. They discovered five planets and charted solar and lunar eclipses. But the true nature of celestial objects awaited the invention of the telescope.

In 1609, hearing of a telescope built by a Dutch eyeglass maker, Italian scientist Galileo Galilei put together his own version, consisting of a convex lens and a concave lens mounted in a lead tube. "Bringing my eye to the concave lens," he noted, "I saw objects satisfactorily large and near." In the next few years, he saw craters on the Moon, sunspots on the Sun, the rings of Saturn, and four moons of Jupiter.

Now, even binoculars will reveal much more than Galileo's instruments, and modern telescopes can see nearly to the edges of the universe. But the cosmos radiates at many more wavelengths than those of visible light. In recent decades, astronomers have developed telescopes that can allow them to see radio waves and microwaves, ultraviolet and infrared radiation, even x-rays and gamma rays—the rest of the spectrum of electromagnetic energy emitted from celestial objects. Satellites above the Earth's obscuring atmosphere provide even clearer images of the universe, and some spacecraft have flown to other planets. There are many ways to look for the mysteries in the cosmos—and there are many mysteries yet to be found.

Inside the movable dome of an observatory, a modern telescope focuses on one of the billions of celestial objects that fill the night sky.

How Do Optical Telescopes Work?

Over the course of four centuries, optical telescopes have captured the light streaming toward Earth from every corner of the universe. These telescopes come in two varieties: refracting, which use lenses to focus light directly into the eyepiece; and reflecting, which bounce light off mirrors before sending it to the eyepiece.

Older telescopes were of the refracting type, but their lenses sagged out of shape when their apertures, or widths, exceeded about 40 inches. Big telescopes, like the Hale telescope shown here, are reflecting. Located on Mount Palomar in California, the Hale telescope, with its 200-inch mirror, can gather a tremendous amount of light. When coupled with an electronic camera, it can see galaxies billions of light-years away.

▲ **The 200-inch Hale** telescope opens to the night sky.

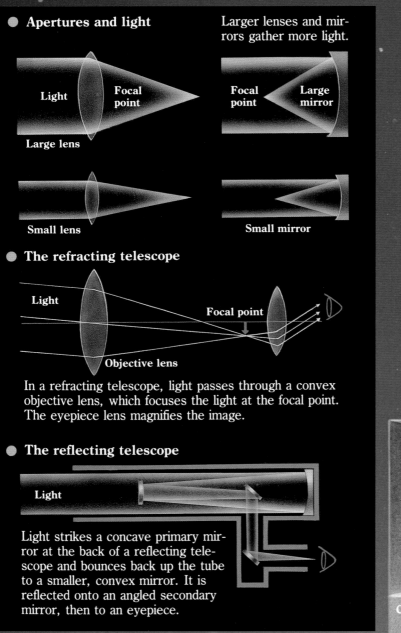

● **Apertures and light** — Larger lenses and mirrors gather more light.

Light — Large lens — Focal point

Focal point — Large mirror

Small lens

Small mirror

● **The refracting telescope**

Light — Focal point — Objective lens

In a refracting telescope, light passes through a convex objective lens, which focuses the light at the focal point. The eyepiece lens magnifies the image.

● **The reflecting telescope**

Light

Light strikes a concave primary mirror at the back of a reflecting telescope and bounces back up the tube to a smaller, convex mirror. It is reflected onto an angled secondary mirror, then to an eyepiece.

Prism

Coudé focus

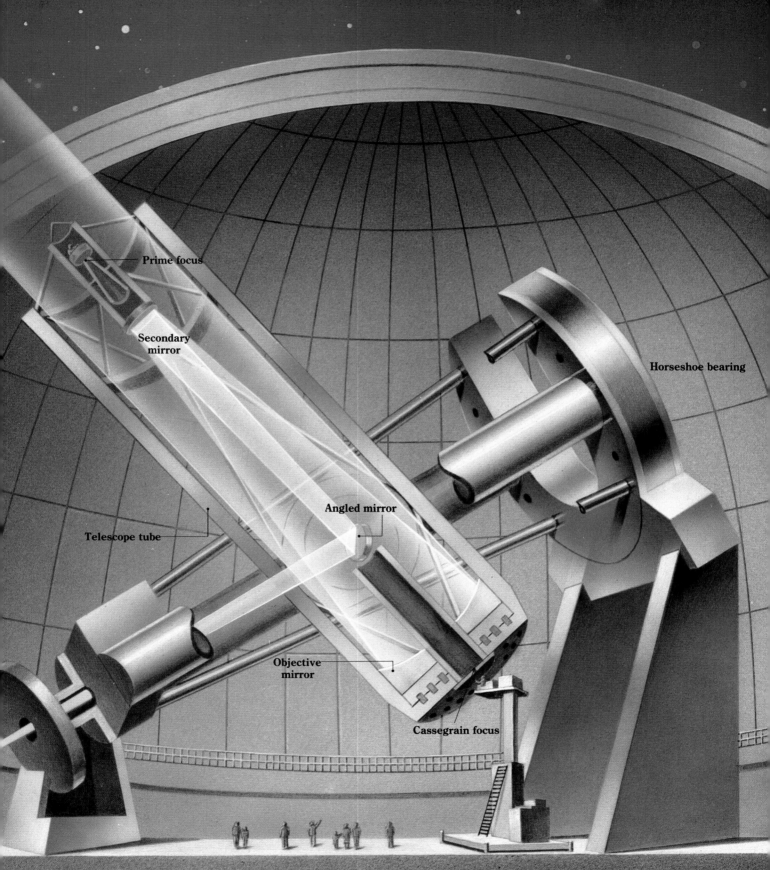

Prime focus

Secondary
mirror

Horseshoe bearing

Angled mirror

Telescope tube

Objective
mirror

Cassegrain focus

Despite great advances in telescope technology in the four decades since it was finished, the Hale telescope is still one of the world's most powerful optical instruments. The big reflector, mounted on a yoke that allows it to rotate, has three main points of focus, each at a different length from the center of the mirror. The prime focus is in a cage at the top of the tube. The Cassegrain focus, which produces large images, is at the bottom of the tube. And the coudé focus is located in a separate room below the telescope. The coudé system makes the telescope especially valuable by spreading starlight into a spectrum, which reveals a star's atmospheric gases and temperature.

How Do Radio Telescopes Work?

In 1937, an American electronic engineer named Grote Reber built a huge, dish-shaped radio receiver in his backyard and with it proved that radio signals were reaching Earth from outer space. Astronomers soon realized that many objects in space, from stars to clouds of dust, gave off radio waves, and that they could learn much about the universe by studying them. So they began designing giant radio dishes to pick up what were otherwise undetectable and invisible cosmic waves.

Radio astronomers must use telescopes that are very different from traditional optical instruments. Radio waves have much longer wavelengths than visible-light waves and, as a result, can only be seen if they are first captured by large, dish-shaped antennas and then converted into electronic signals. The most important part of a radio telescope is the huge dish, usually more than 100 feet across, that captures the signals and, like the primary mirror of a reflecting telescope, focuses them on an electronic receiver. The receiver beams the signals to a computer, which translates them into pictures and graphs that astronomers can understand.

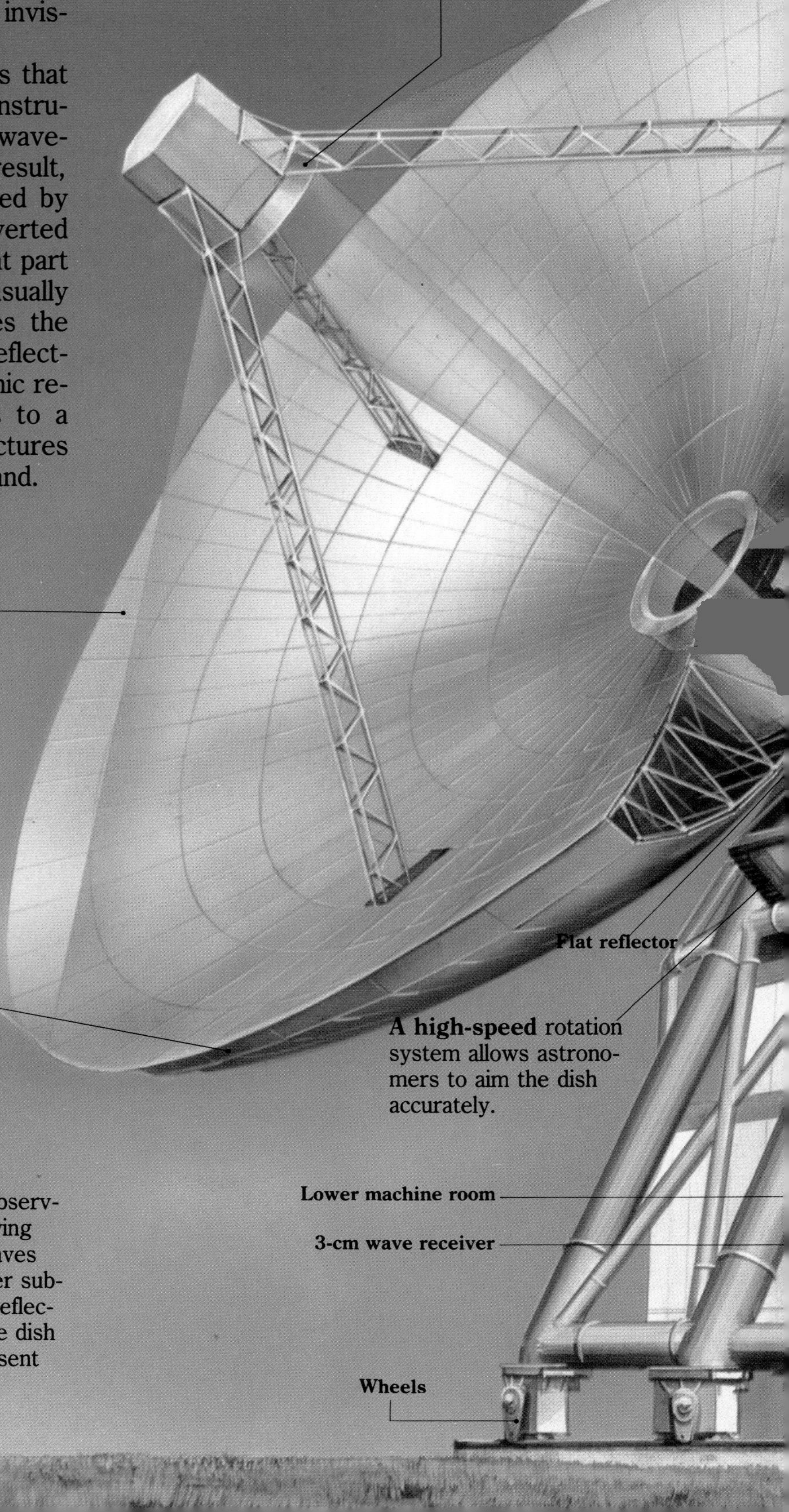

The subreflector is held in place at the main dish focus. It reflects waves from the main dish down to receivers in the base of the telescope.

The interior of the dish, also known as the main reflector, is covered with 600 mirrored panels made of a lightweight, highly heat-resistant material. The curved dish focuses radio waves on the subreflector.

The framework of the dish has a plate to keep the dish at a stable temperature, preventing signal distortion.

Flat reflector

A high-speed rotation system allows astronomers to aim the dish accurately.

Lower machine room

3-cm wave receiver

Wheels

■ **Capturing radio waves**

The radio telescope at Japan's Nobeyama Radio Observatory *(shown here)* has a curved, 147-foot dish, giving scientists detailed images of the cosmos. Radio waves strike the large dish and are bounced to the smaller subreflector held above the dish by trusses. The subreflector sends radio waves down the open center of the dish to a receiver. The signals are strengthened, then sent to a computer that creates an image or a graph.

● When telescopes join forces

Because radio waves have such long wavelengths, it is hard to get detailed images using a single dish. To overcome the problem, scientists use interferometry, in which two or more radio telescopes far from each other look at the same object at the same time. A computer combines the data (so that the waves "interfere" with each other). The resulting image appears to have been made with one enormous radio telescope. Telescopes on several continents can be combined this way, creating a dish that seems almost as big as the Earth.

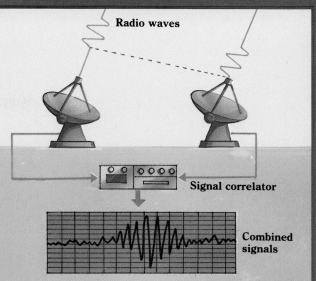

Radio waves

Signal correlator

Combined signals

The flat secondary mirror picks up signals from the concave reflector. The secondary mirror is computer controlled so it can guide radio waves very precisely.

Radio signals make their way from the secondary mirror to the receivers.

▲ **A spectroscope** analyzes radio waves.

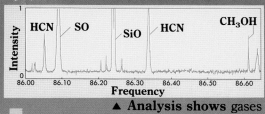

▲ **Analysis shows** gases in the Orion nebula.

No. 6 concave mirror

Signal receivers, cooled so they will not pick up stray radio noise, collect several radio wavelengths.

No. 4 concave mirror   No. 3 concave mirror   No. 5 concave mirror

▲ **A computer** displays the gases in color.

How Do Astronomers Study the Sun?

It is only an average star, yet the Sun provides life-giving heat and light to Earth by burning more than 4 million tons of gases each second at temperatures reaching millions of degrees Fahrenheit. The home star gives off energy in so many different ways that it is only during the past 40 years that scientists have begun to understand its nature.

Because it radiates in many wavelengths, the Sun cannot be completely studied by one instrument alone. For instance, astronomers would use an optical telescope to look at the visible light given off by lower-temperature gases near the solar surface. Radio telescopes might study the movement of gases into the corona. Each wavelength range reveals new details. Optical and radio telescopes, satellites, and special solar observatories all contribute data about the Sun.

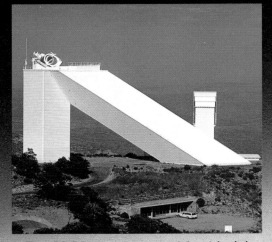

▲ The McMath telescope (*above*) in Arizona, with its 492-foot shaft burrowing into the ground, is the largest solar observatory in the world.

● **Radio telescopes**

Radio telescopes see the long-wavelength waves that make up the radio end of the spectrum. For instance, they can observe the radiation given off by hot gases moving in the corona.

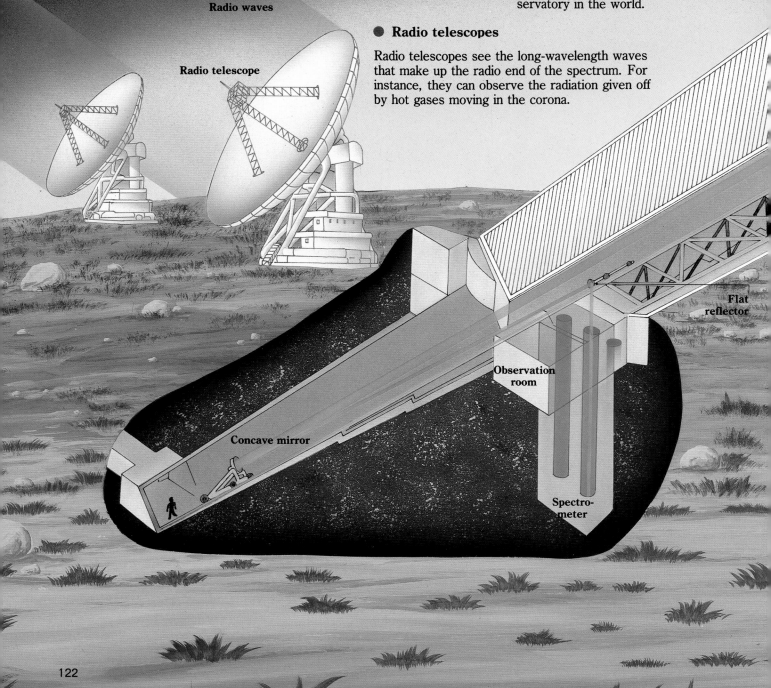

Radio waves

Radio telescope

Flat reflector

Observation room

Concave mirror

Spectrometer

Satellites

Solar ultraviolet and x-ray emissions have shorter wavelengths that cannot pass through the Earth's atmosphere. These forms of radiation can only be studied by mounting small telescopes on rockets and satellites.

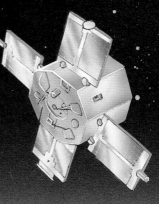

Sunlight

Tower telescope

Flat mirror

The McMath solar telescope

Observing details of the blazing Sun requires a specially designed telescope, such as the Mc-Math *(left)*. To focus on areas just 100 miles wide, the telescope must have an extremely long focal length, and the McMath is the size of a 50-story building laid on its side. The 11-story tower (above ground) allows sunlight to enter undisturbed by air turbulence near the ground. The light strikes a movable mirror that follows the Sun, then is beamed to a concave mirror at the bottom of the shaft. From there it is reflected to another mirror and finally to the observing room.

Coronagraph

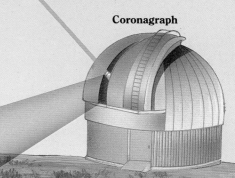

Coronagraph

A coronagraph *(above)* is a special kind of optical telescope that lets astronomers see the Sun's thin upper atmosphere, or corona. Because the corona can only be seen when the brilliant light from the Sun's surface is blocked out, the coronagraph has a disk in its tube that creates an artificial eclipse.

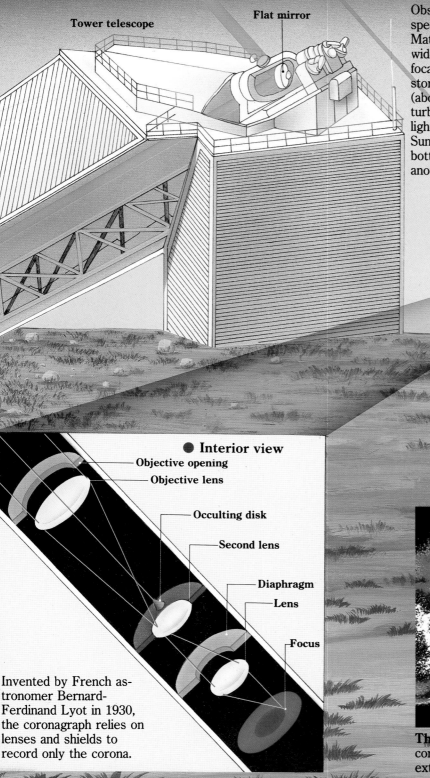

Interior view

- Objective opening
- Objective lens
- Occulting disk
- Second lens
- Diaphragm
- Lens
- Focus

Invented by French astronomer Bernard-Ferdinand Lyot in 1930, the coronagraph relies on lenses and shields to record only the corona.

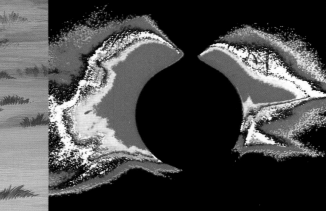

The Sun's corona, as photographed by a coronagraph from Skylab in 1973. The corona extends twice the Sun's diameter into space.

Hundreds of artificial satellites have leapt into orbit since the Soviet Union launched Sputnik in 1957. These machines have dramatically changed humanity's views both of the universe and of Earth itself.

Satellites and probes fall into three groups: those that observe the Earth, those that peer into space, and spacecraft that travel to other planets in our solar system. Satellites can have a great impact on human life as they keep track of the planet's weather and environment and as they provide fast telephone, TV, and radio communications. Other satellites are astronomical observatories, looking at distant stars and galaxies. Free of the Earth's blanketing atmosphere, satellites can study cosmic rays and high-frequency radiation from deep space, learning about supernovas and neutron stars. Probes to other planets provide pictures and measurements of the strange worlds nearby.

The Infrared Astronomical Satellite, launched in 1983 by the United States and the European Space Agency, studied cosmic infrared radiation.

Despite flaws in its optical systems, the Hubble Space Telescope, launched in 1990, may see objects 50 times fainter than those seen by the best ground-based telescopes.

■ Beyond the wall of air

Earth's atmosphere allows only radio, visible-light, and some infrared and ultraviolet waves to reach the Earth's surface from space. To see celestial x-rays, gamma rays, and most infrared and ultraviolet radiation, scientists must get above the Earth's protective atmosphere. In the past, high-flying airplanes, special balloons, and small rockets were used. Now, orbiting satellites give scientists a steady window on the sky.

Infrared observatory

Radio observatory

Optical observatory

In 1976, *Viking 1* landed on Mars. The craft and its successor, *Viking 2*, analyzed soil for simple life forms. No life was found, but the soil did contain water, as well as iron oxides, sulfur, and carbon.

On a remarkable tour of the Solar System, *Voyager 2*, launched in 1977, visited all of the outer planets except Pluto.

The Mariner series launched 10 planetary probes in the 1960s and 1970s. The spacecraft flew near Mercury, Venus, and Mars.

● **Planetary probes**

Probes to other planets have dramatically increased our understanding of the Solar System. Two American craft landed on Mars; two Soviet craft survived briefly on the very hot surface of Venus. At least one craft has flown close to all of the planets except Pluto.

Tenma, a Japanese x-ray observatory, is designed to look closely at violent, energetic objects in space such as black holes and supernovas.

The International Ultraviolet Explorer (IUE), a joint American and European satellite launched in 1978, sees radiation from interstellar gas and white dwarf stars.

What Is a Planetarium?

A planetarium is the universe brought indoors. Stars, planets, and other celestial images are projected up onto a dome by a sophisticated machine that is actually a group of projectors that work in combination. Designed to show the heavens as they appear from Earth, planetariums are also time machines. They can show star patterns as they were thousands of years ago and as they will be in coming centuries. Planetariums can also show the night sky as it appears from the Northern and the Southern hemispheres. Constellations such as the Southern Cross, not visible in North America, appear realistically on the dome.

The first modern planetariums were built in the 1920s by the Carl Zeiss optical company. By the 1990s, they were often used with computers, sound and video projectors, and other technologically advanced systems to immerse the viewer completely in the feeling of being in outer space. The most recently designed planetariums can even simulate flights to other stars.

▶ **One turn** of the planetarium's drive shaft is equivalent to the movement of a planet or star in one day.

● **The Zeiss planetarium**

Spheres at the ends of the dumbbell-shaped Zeiss planetarium *(above)* project the stars of the Northern and Southern hemispheres. The planets are projected from the structure connecting the spheres. Coordinated gears rotate the planetarium, allowing the machine to show the daily and yearly changes in appearance of the sky.

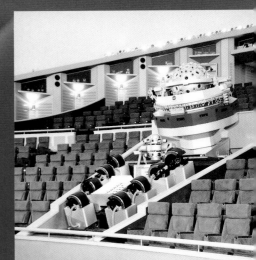

▲ **Infinium,** a newer, sophisticated planetarium, makes use of a single-sphere star projector at the Tsukuba Expo Center in Japan.

Constellation projector

Northern stars projectors

After 60 years of gradual improvement,
planetariums changed dramatically in
the early 1980s. Aided by computers,
planetariums such as the Minolta optical projector below can show trips to
stars hundreds of light-years from
Earth. Older machines were earth-
bound, but new technology allows planetariums to show the universe as it
would appear from the surface of Mars
or the other planets.

Mercury discharge tubes

Bright star projector

Slip ring

Ecliptic projector

Comet projector

Milky Way projector

Saturn projector

Sun projector

Moon projector

Mercury projector

Venus projector

Mars projector

Jupiter projector

8

Life in Space

Space travel and exploration were only a dream until October 4, 1957, when the Soviet Union launched Sputnik, the first artificial satellite to orbit the Earth. Since that day, more than 3,000 spacecraft have circled the globe and dozens of unpiloted probes have been sent to visit the Moon, fly by Halley's comet, and explore most planets in the Solar System.

If humans are to follow in the paths of those probes, an orbital space station would make a good jumping-off point. Spacecraft launched from such a platform would not have to overcome Earth's gravity to begin their journey. The parts needed to build the station could be carried into orbit by the space shuttle, whose design and operation are discussed on pages 130-133. Already, 15 countries have volunteered to help with the space station's construction.

The next step—the colonization of space—would be even more exciting with hundreds of thousands of former Earth residents living on moons and planets scattered across the Solar System. A journey beyond the planets would be the most ambitious undertaking of all. *Voyager 2,* a pilotless probe launched from Earth in 1977, passed Neptune in 1989 and will take another 10 years just to reach the edge of the Solar System. Space travelers of the future—provided they could move at one-tenth the speed of light, or 18,600 miles per second—would still need at least 45 years to voyage from Earth to Proxima Centauri, the Sun's nearest star.

Able to ferry astronauts, satellites, and space-station supplies into Earth orbit, the space shuttle—shown preparing for reentry, with its cargo bay doors closed—has been an important step in the exploration of space.

How Does the Space Shuttle Work?

The space shuttle has three distinct modes of flight. At liftoff, when it weighs about 2,200 tons, the craft soars vertically into the sky. Propelling it are twin booster rockets and an external fuel tank. The boosters burn solid fuel; the tank supplies liquid fuel for combustion in the shuttle's three main on-board engines. After the booster rockets have consumed their last ounce of fuel—about two minutes after liftoff—they are jettisoned and fall to the ocean below.

Shortly before the spacecraft reaches orbit, the fuel in the external tank runs out and the tank is released. One of the few nonreusable parts on the shuttle, the tank burns up as it falls back through the atmosphere. In orbit, the craft assumes an "upside-down" orientation—its cargo doors opened toward Earth—unless it is launching a satellite.

To prepare for landing, the shuttle—now weighing as little as 94 tons—is turned so that its engines face in the direction of its flight. The engines are then fired to slow the ship. After turning again so that its bottom surface is toward the ground, the craft enters the atmosphere. Cruising earthward as a glider, the shuttle touches down at about 220 miles an hour.

③ **Nine minutes** into the flight, the external fuel tank runs dry and is dropped.

④ **Freed of its fuel** tank, the shuttle climbs to an orbital altitude of 175 miles above the Earth.

Atmospheric limit

The jettisoned external fuel tank, because of its large cross section, generates such friction as it falls through the atmosphere that it burns up during descent.

② **About two minutes** after liftoff, the boosters burn out and are thrown to either side.

① **As its three** main engines and two booster rockets fire, the shuttle lifts off.

Each booster rocket sprouts three parachutes, then lands in the ocean for recovery.

● Profile of a workhorse

At launch, the space shuttle—often called the orbiter—is buttressed by a huge external fuel tank and two slender booster rockets. The reusable boosters carry about 500 tons of solid fuel each; although these reserves burn out in just two minutes, they create 6.6 million pounds of thrust. The orbiter's three main engines burn a mix of supercooled liquid oxygen and hydrogen, which are kept separate in the external fuel tank and combined under high pressure in a combustion chamber for ignition. Two smaller tail engines make directional changes.

External liquid-fuel tank

Solid-fuel booster rocket

Orbiter

⑤ **In orbit,** the cargo bay doors are opened to prepare for launching of a satellite and to let the heat inside the crew's living quarters radiate away.

⑥ **As a first step** in its touchdown sequence, the shuttle is pivoted until its two small course-correction engines point forward. The engines are then fired in short bursts, slowing the spacecraft from 17,000 to 8,000 miles per hour.

⑦ **As the shuttle** enters the atmosphere, air friction heats its underside to 2,700° F.

⑧ **Nearing** the ground, the shuttle executes several wide S-turns that help slow it even further. These and the spacecraft's angle of descent are controlled by computers.

⑨ **The landing** wheels emerge about 20 seconds before touchdown.

131

Is It Hard to Live in Zero Gravity?

A spacecraft must be a little pocket of Earth's environment, sealed against the frigid void of space. Inside this snug shelter, astronauts try to go about their daily lives much as if they were still on Earth. Unbound by the planet's gravity, however, the astronauts are weightless; eating, sleeping, and exercising therefore present special problems. But engineers have worked out solutions for each.

Because crumbs would scatter off a plate in space, food that breaks apart easily must be ground into a paste and then sucked through a tube. More solid foods, by contrast, are served on plates. A typical shuttle meal features a shrimp cocktail, steak and broccoli, pudding, and grape juice.

When sleeping, the astronauts are held in place by straps or they use a sleeping bag attached to a bunk. Without these restraints, they would float and bump into cabin walls.

Exercise is a special concern because muscles that are not forced to work against gravity can become flabby. Astronauts work out on bikes or treadmills for about 30 minutes a day.

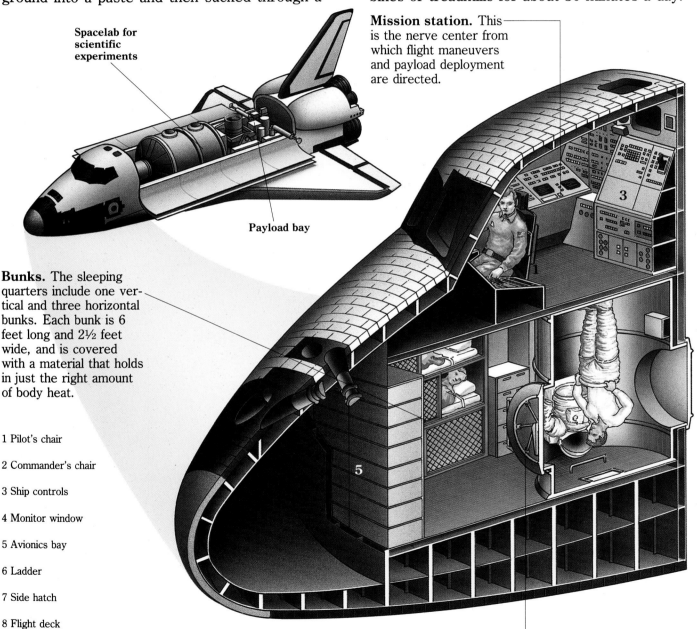

Spacelab for scientific experiments

Payload bay

Mission station. This is the nerve center from which flight maneuvers and payload deployment are directed.

Bunks. The sleeping quarters include one vertical and three horizontal bunks. Each bunk is 6 feet long and 2½ feet wide, and is covered with a material that holds in just the right amount of body heat.

1 Pilot's chair

2 Commander's chair

3 Ship controls

4 Monitor window

5 Avionics bay

6 Ladder

7 Side hatch

8 Flight deck

9 Mid-deck

10 Lower deck

Air lock. A cylindrical chamber that can be sealed off from the rest of the craft, the air lock has enough room for two astronauts to change into and out of their spacesuits before and after a spacewalk.

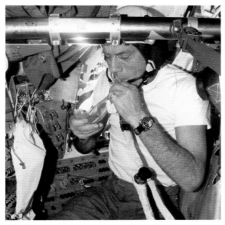

Eating. Astronaut Deke Slayton enjoys a meal of ground-up food sucked through a straw. Meat, fruit, and candy are left whole.

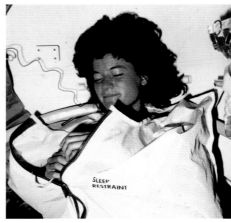

Sleeping. Snug as a bug in a bag, shuttle astronaut Sally Ride takes a space nap in a lightweight sleeping envelope lashed to her bunk.

Exercising. Astronaut Pete Conrad works out in orbit on a stationary exercise bike that keeps his lower-body muscles from growing weak.

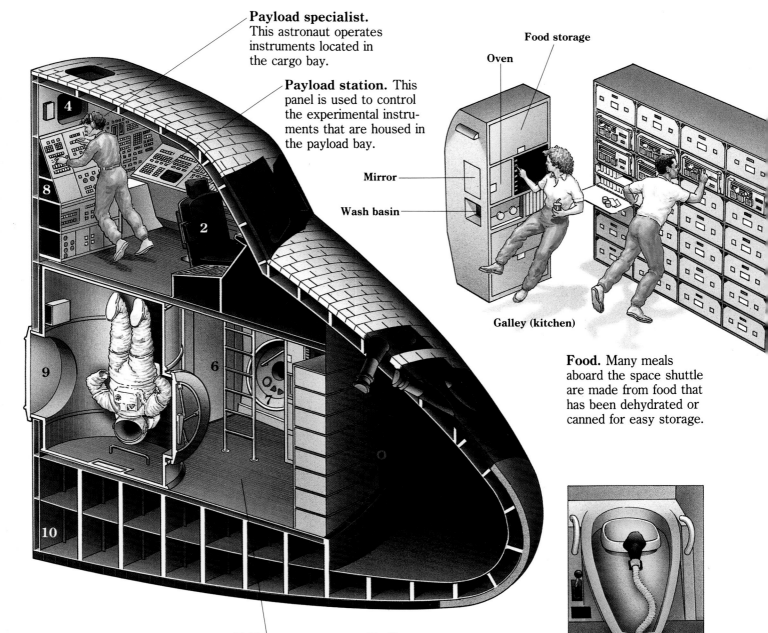

Payload specialist. This astronaut operates instruments located in the cargo bay.

Payload station. This panel is used to control the experimental instruments that are housed in the payload bay.

Mirror

Wash basin

Oven

Food storage

Galley (kitchen)

Food. Many meals aboard the space shuttle are made from food that has been dehydrated or canned for easy storage.

Toilet compartment. Bodily wastes are sucked down by a vacuum. Solid waste is dried and sterilized for disposal on Earth. Liquids go to a wastewater tank.

Toilet

What Is It Like to Wear a Spacesuit?

A spacesuit has to work like an airtight coat of armor. It must protect the astronaut from temperatures of 300° F. below zero to 300° F. above. It must shield the astronaut from the vacuum of space, where low pressure would allow blood to boil. And it must be able to deflect or impede the micrometeoroids that could otherwise rip through the suit with fatal effect.

A spacesuit must also be as gentle as it is tough. For the astronaut to perform delicate re-pair tasks outside the spacecraft, the suit must be flexible. To allow the astronaut to work in space for extended periods, the suit must provide breathable air and a comfortable, constant inside temperature. And so that the astronaut does not dehydrate while working, the suit must contain a source of drinking water.

Meeting these dictates can result in a space-suit that weighs 250 pounds—on Earth, that is. In space, the suit weighs next to nothing.

Suited for spacewalking

Helmet. A transparent gold film on the visor reflects 60 percent of the sunlight that hits it, keeping the helmet cool and minimizing glare.

Portable Life-Support Subsystem (PLSS)

Life support. Bolted onto the astronaut's back is a complex and bulky, but essential, pack known as the Portable Life-Support Subsystem, or PLSS. It circulates oxygen for breathing and water for cooling. It also carries away perspiration and exhaled carbon dioxide.

Spacesuits

To protect against micrometeoroids, the spacesuit's outer skin is made of seven layers of tough woven plastic fibers. The inner layers contain aluminum and rubber for insulation.

Communications gear—including a two-way radio and a heart monitor—is in the top and bottom of each pack.

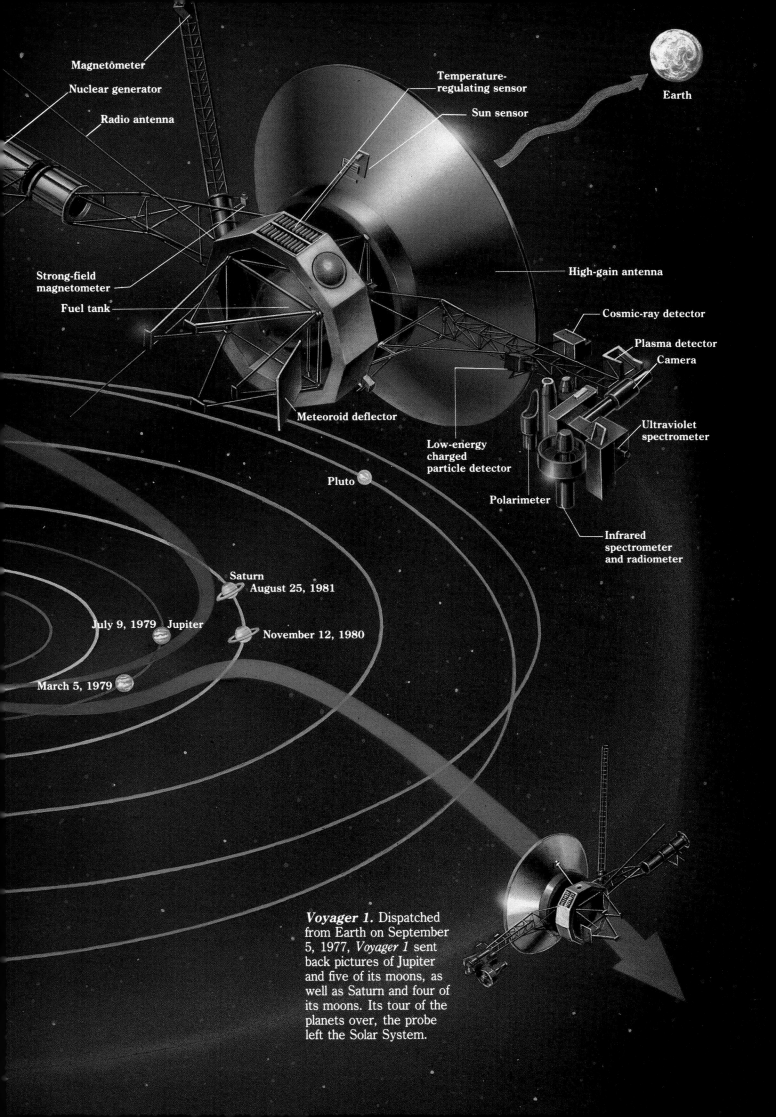

Magnetometer

Nuclear generator

Radio antenna

Strong-field magnetometer

Fuel tank

Meteoroid deflector

Temperature-regulating sensor

Sun sensor

Earth

High-gain antenna

Cosmic-ray detector

Plasma detector

Camera

Low-energy charged particle detector

Ultraviolet spectrometer

Pluto

Polarimeter

Infrared spectrometer and radiometer

Saturn
August 25, 1981

July 9, 1979 Jupiter

November 12, 1980

March 5, 1979

Voyager 1. Dispatched from Earth on September 5, 1977, *Voyager 1* sent back pictures of Jupiter and five of its moons, as well as Saturn and four of its moons. Its tour of the planets over, the probe left the Solar System.

How Would a Space Colony Look?

Space colonies have been mainstays of science fiction for decades. But with world population growing at an alarming rate, the idea of a second home in space could soon change from a futuristic fantasy to an urgent necessity.

Already, a number of visionary scientists have drawn up plans for off-Earth habitats. Two of their more feasible designs are shown on these pages.

To re-create the sensation of Earth's gravity, both of the envisioned colonies would spin about a central axis; the resulting centrifugal force would gently press the occupants against the outer walls. The doughnut shape, known as a torus, resembles a mile-wide bicycle wheel floating in space; it would house up to 10,000 colonists. The gigantic cylinder at right could hold 200 to 300 times that many.

A pie in the sky

The torus design *(below)* features a tubular rim connected to a hub by spokes housing elevators. Reflective panels and a tilted mirror supply light and heat.

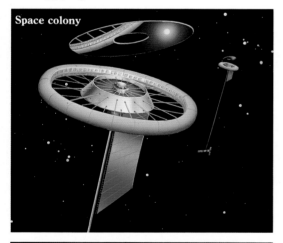

Space colony

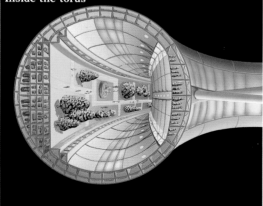

Inside the torus

■ A cylinder in space

Space farms

Shuttle carrying cargo and colonists

This 20-mile-long cylindrical space colony, dreamed up by physicist Gerard O'Neill, would provide living space for two to three million inhabitants. Lakes, farmland, and towns would occupy three strips running the length of the cylinder. During the "day," mirrors would reflect sunlight into the colony through windows placed between the strips. At "night," the mirrors would cover the windows and block the Sun.

With the structure spinning about its axis, the outer rim would be the ground. To colonists looking "up"—or toward the axis—buildings, rivers, and mountains on the opposite wall would seem to hang from the sky.

Antenna

Earth

Window

Residential section

Strip of land

M.K

Can Humans Get to Other Planets?

Rockets launched from Earth use up most of their fuel just to escape the planet's gravity, so they would make inefficient vehicles for a voyage to other planets. A spacecraft launched from a platform orbiting the Earth, however, would need very little thrust to achieve escape velocity.

Scientists are seeking ways of delivering that thrust. One possibility is an engine fueled by ions—that is, by atoms that have gained or lost one or more electrons.

Like a motor scooter that cannot climb hills but gets good gas mileage on the straightaway, an ion engine would be useless for blastoff but could push heavy loads through the weak gravity of space on mere sips—or nibbles—of fuel. About 500 pounds of the metal cesium, for example, could drive a 1,500-ton spacecraft through interplanetary space for as long as two years.

Space station
in near-Earth orbit

Payload

Body of
ion-powered
spacecraft

Heat radiator

Solar panels

Inside an ion engine

An ion engine uses electricity to produce thrust. In the first step of the process, fuel flows to an ionizer, where an electric charge tears electrons from the fuel atoms. This creates ions—atoms with a positive electrical charge—and free electrons, which have a negative charge. In step two, an electrified double screen attracts, then violently repels the ions, flinging them out of the engine and thrusting the vehicle forward. In step three, neutralizers expel electrons into the path of the ions. The electrons and ions recombine in space, keeping the spacecraft from becoming electrically charged itself.

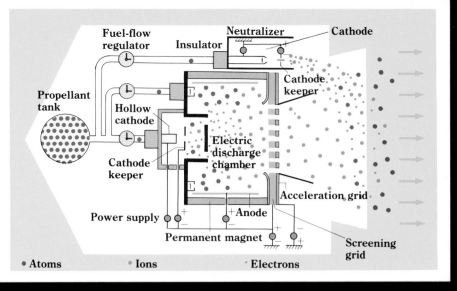

Fuel-flow regulator

Neutralizer

Cathode

Insulator

Propellant tank

Cathode keeper

Hollow cathode

Electric discharge chamber

Cathode keeper

Acceleration grid

Power supply

Anode

Permanent magnet

Screening grid

• Atoms   • Ions   • Electrons

A transport driven by ions

Ion engines

In this vision of the future, a spacecraft powered by 14 ion engines *(above)* ferries materials between a space station *(left)* in low Earth orbit and a space colony *(right)* being constructed far above it. The "wings" of the craft are solar panels. These collect the Sun's radiation, which is converted into electricity for the engines.

A pilotless probe propelled by two ion engines heads for other planets. Although the engines would increase velocity by just 20 miles per hour on the first day, the probe would eventually be boosted by 10,000 miles per hour.

Space colony in high orbit

Where Next?

In 1986, less than three decades after the first artificial satellite orbited the Earth, a new era in space exploration dawned with the launch of the Soviet space station Mir (Russian for "peace"). By 1988, when a two-person crew returned from Mir after a record 366 days in space, the space platform had proved that humans can live in space for the duration of an interplanetary voyage. A round trip to Mars, for example, would require at least 14 months' travel time.

Such a journey would be a great logistical challenge. A spacefarer consumes 2.2 pounds of oxygen, 1.3 pounds of food, and 6 pounds of water each day, so a five-member crew bound for Mars would need nearly 9 tons of supplies for life support alone. Space scientists have therefore suggested breaking the mission into two parts. A cargo ship would transport food, fuel, and exploration gear to Mars, where it would rendezvous in orbit with a second vessel carrying the human crew. From this base, which might grow to the size of a space station (below), the astronauts could explore Mars—and some day its neighboring planets.

A meeting of machines

Ending its 50-million-mile journey from Earth, an interplanetary explorer craft (above) prepares to dock with a space station (right) orbiting some 250 miles above Mars (below). At the space station, the astronauts would find a smaller, specialized vehicle in which they could descend to the surface of the red planet. After a few weeks of reconnoitering, the astronauts would return to the explorer to begin their six-month journey home.

Space station

Bases in space will serve as launch pads for future explorations.

Glossary

Absorption lines: Dark lines on a spectrum that occur when light is absorbed between the source, for example a star, and the observer. Each element absorbs light at particular wavelengths.

Accretion: A process by which matter coalesces through collision and gravity and builds up into a larger object. The planets are thought to have formed by accretion in the solar nebula.

Accretion disk: A rapidly spinning disk of hot gas and dust surrounding and being drawn into a star, a black hole, or a neutron star.

Aphelion: The point in an object's orbit around the Sun where it is farthest from the Sun.

Apogee: The point in an object's orbit around the Earth where it is farthest from the Earth.

Asteroids: Small rocky bodies orbiting the Sun in a wide belt between Mars and Jupiter; also known as minor planets.

Aurora: Light given off when energetic charged particles from the solar wind become trapped in a planet's magnetic field and collide with atmospheric gases near the planet's magnetic poles.

Axis: The imaginary line, drawn through the poles of a celestial body, around which the body spins.

Basalt: A type of rock formed from volcanic lava, commonly found on Earth, in lunar maria, and probably on Mars.

Big Bang: According to theory, the explosion about 15 billion years ago that started the expansion of the universe.

Big Crunch: The predicted fate of the universe, if there is enough mass and thus strong enough gravity to halt the expansion of the universe and cause it to collapse into a giant fireball.

Centrifugal force: An imaginary force that appears to pull an object outward from the center of a circular path.

Charged particles: Basic units of matter, such as electrons and protons, that are responsible for all electrical and chemical reactions; they have either a positive (+) or negative (−) charge; like charges repel, unlike charges attract.

Coma: A region of gas and dust that surrounds the nucleus of a comet and forms the comet's visible head.

Comet: A small body of ice and dust that orbits the Sun, usually in an elongated orbit; when approaching the Sun, ice vaporizes and forms a head and tail.

Constellation: A group of stars that appears to form a picture and mark an area of the sky, as seen from Earth. There are 88 constellations that divide up the sky.

Core: The central region of a celestial body. In stars nuclear fusion reactions occur in the core. In planets the core is usually composed of dense, hot, solid matter.

Corona: The outer layer of the Sun's atmosphere composed of thin, hot gases that has been stripped of electrons; the solar corona expands continuously beyond the Sun to become the solar wind. The corona is visible only during a total eclipse or with a special solar telescope called a coronagraph. Also, the outermost atmosphere of a comet extending millions of miles beyond the nucleus.

Cosmic rays: Charged particles moving close to the speed of light, thought to be a product of supernova explosions or other violent events.

Craters: Indentations on the surface of planets and moons formed by the impact of meteorites, or the sunken area around the opening of a volcano.

Crust: The solid surface layer of a moon or planet.

Deuteron: A particle containing one proton and one neutron, produced in nuclear fusion reaction.

Doppler effect: Light and sound waves appear to change wavelength, or frequency, according to whether the source is moving toward or away from the observer.

Ecliptic: The apparent annual path of the Sun against the background stars; the plane of Earth's orbit.

Electromagnetic radiation: A flow of energy that is produced when electrically charged bodies, such as electrons, are accelerated. It travels at the speed of light, and can be thought of as either a wave or as particles, known as photons.

Electromagnetic spectrum: The range of frequencies of electromagnetic radiation from low frequency, long wavelength radio waves, through infrared radiation, visible light, ultraviolet rays, to high frequency, short wavelength x-rays and gamma rays.

Electron: A negatively charged particle that normally orbits an atom's nucleus, but may be set free by ionization processes.

Elementary particle: The smallest component of matter and energy.

Emission lines: Bright lines on a spectrum that are produced when very hot gases around the source emit light at specific wavelengths.

Escape velocity: The minimum speed required for an object to overcome a celestial object's gravitational pull.

Exotic particles: Particles that can only exist on their own under conditions of extreme pressure, such as during the Big Bang and in the core of neutron stars.

Galaxy: A collection of stars, gas, and dust that may contain anywhere from millions to hundreds of billions of stars held together by the mutual gravity of its members. Our galaxy is the Milky Way.

Gravitational lens: A massive object, such as a galaxy, lying between the Earth and a distant object, often a quasar. The gravitational field of the lens bends the light of the distant object and produces two or more magnified and distorted images of the distant object.

Gravitational waves: A form of radiation predicted by the theory of general relativity; produced when massive objects are accelerated or disturbed, such as with vibrating black holes or supernovas.

Gravity: The force responsible for the attraction of one mass to another; one of the fundamental forces of nature.

Hertzsprung-Russell diagram: A chart of the relationship between the brightness and the spectral type (or surface temperature) of stars.

Hydrogen: The most common element in the universe. Neutral hydrogen contains one electron and one proton; ionized hydrogen is positively charged hydrogen atoms from which the electrons have been stripped; molecular hydrogen is a two-atom molecule of hydrogen.

Ion: An atom that has lost or gained one or more electrons. A positive ion of an element has fewer electrons orbiting the nucleus than a neutral atom, a negative ion has more.

Kelvin: A temperature scale that sets 0 at absolute zero degrees (−459.69° F.).

Light-year: An astronomical unit of distance equal to the distance light travels in a vacuum in one year, or 5.9 trillion miles.

LMC/SMC: Large Magellanic Cloud/Small Magellanic Cloud—the galaxies nearest to the Milky Way.

Magma: Melted rock formed beneath the surface of a planet.

Magnetic field: A region in which a compass would respond to the magnetism of a body. Earth's weak magnetic field can swing a compass needle. In astronomical bodies, the field can be more than one million million times stronger. Magnetism is one of the fundamental forces of nature.

Magnetic field lines: Lines of magnetic force that tend to run from one magnetic pole to another on the planets, but become twisted on the Sun in active regions producing sunspots.

Magnetometer: An instrument used to measure the strength and direction of a magnetic field.

Magnitude: The brightness of an object relative to other objects; **apparent magnitude** refers to the brightness of an object seen from Earth; **absolute magnitude** refers to the brightness of an object at a standard distance from Earth.

Main sequence: A diagonal region on the Hertzsprung-Russell diagram that includes 90% of all stars.

Mantle: The layer of a planet between the core and the crust.

Metallic hydrogen: A form of hydrogen that occurs under high pressure, such as in the core of planets where it is thought to have properties similar to mercury. Metallic water is also thought to form under extreme pressure.

Meteoroids: Small metallic or rocky bodies orbiting the Sun; once they enter Earth's atmosphere they are called **meteors;** those that strike a planet's surface are known as **meteorites. Micrometeoroids** are interplanetary dust particles that travel at high velocities.

Nebula: A cloud of interstellar gas and dust; often the birthplace of stars or the remains of a dying star.

Neutrino: A chargeless, subatomic particle with little or no mass; a by-product of nuclear fusion processes that occur in stars.

Neutron: An uncharged particle with a mass similar to a proton's, found in the nucleus of all elements except hydrogen.

Nodes: The two points in a celestial object's orbit that cross a reference plane. When an object orbiting the Sun crosses the plane, such as the Sun's equatorial plane or the plane of the ecliptic, it passes through the **ascending node** when it travels from south to north. When it crosses the plane moving from north to south it passes through the **descending node.**

Nuclear fission: The splitting of a nucleus resulting in the release of large amounts of energy.

Nuclear fusion: The combining of two atomic nuclei to form a heavier nucleus, releasing enormous amounts of energy as a by-product. In stars two hydrogen nuclei fuse to form helium.

Nucleosynthesis: The creation of elements heavier than hydrogen and helium by nuclear reactions.

Nucleus: The massive center of an atom, composed of protons and neutrons and orbited by electrons. The ice-rock core of a comet; the central region of a galaxy.

Objective lens: The lens or system of lenses in a refracting telescope that brings light to a focus.

Orbit: The path of an object revolving around another object, determined by the laws of gravity and motion.

Ozone: An unstable three-atom form of the element oxygen, which normally occurs as a two-atom molecule. In the Earth's atmosphere it absorbs the incoming rays of harmful ultraviolet radiation.

Parallax: A measurement of stellar distance. A star's apparent motion relative to background stars over a six-month period, the greater the change in position, the nearer the star.

Particle: The smallest part of matter; the elementary particles within an atom, such as electrons, protons, and neutrons; the smallest component of a gas, atoms, and molecules; or the smallest forms of solid matter in space, interstellar and interplanetary dust particles.

Payload: Cargo carried by a spacecraft related to the purpose of the flight and not necessary for its operation.

Perigee: The point in the orbit of an object around the Earth where it is closest to the Earth.

Perihelion: The point in the orbit of an object around the Sun where it is closest to the Sun.

Planet: A large body that is held in orbit about a star by gravity and shines only with reflected light.

Planetesimals: Small primitive bodies that orbited the newborn Sun in the solar nebula; the building blocks of planets.

Plasma: A gas made up of charged particles; considered to be a fourth state of matter along with gases, liquids, and solids.

Polarimeter: An instrument that measures the polarization (or direction of vibration) of light.

Positron: A particle having the same mass as an electron, but an equal and opposite (positive) electrical charge.

Proto-: Refers to an object that has not completed its formation process, such as the proto-Earth, protostar, and protosun.

Proton: A positively charged particle with about 2,000 times the mass of an electron; normally found in an atom's nucleus.

Reflector: A mirror used to collect and focus radiation; a telescope that uses mirrors to collect and focus light.

Refractor: A lens used to focus radiation; a telescope that uses lenses to collect and focus light.

Revolution: Moving in a curved path around a center.

Rotation: Turning or spinning about on an axis or center.

Shock waves: A sharp increase in pressure, density, and temperature traveling like a wave through a medium; shock waves occur when a disturbance cannot be dispersed quickly enough and begins to pile up.

Solar System: The Sun, the planets, asteroids, comets, and other bodies that orbit the Sun; a star and the objects that are in orbit around it.

Solar wind: A continuous stream of charged particles, originating in the Sun's corona, that flows outward from the Sun through the Solar System.

Spectral type: A star's classification based on its surface temperature, or spectrum.

Spectrograph: An instrument that can be attached to a telescope to record a photographic image of a spectrum; one of the most important tools astronomers use to study celestial objects.

Spectrum (pl. spectra): The rainbow sequence of colors, or frequencies, that forms when visible light is separated into its components, ranging from long wavelength red to short wavelength purple; often banded with absorption or emission lines.

Subatomic particle: Any particle smaller than an atom, from atomic components such as protons to parts of protons.

Sunspots: Dark spots on the surface of the Sun caused by distortions in magnetic field lines. The number of sunspots grows and shrinks in an 11-year cycle.

Superfluid: A liquid that has no resistance to flow, it can even flow upward. A superfluid of neutrons is thought to exist in the core of neutron stars.

Thrust: The force that propels a rocket or spacecraft.

Tidal forces: A force resulting from different gravitational pull on opposite sides of an object.

Index

Staff for
UNDERSTANDING SCIENCE AND NATURE

Editorial Directors: Patricia Daniels, Karin Kinney
Text Editor: Allan Fallow
Writer: Mark Galan
Assistant Editor/Research: Elizabeth Thompson
Editorial Assistant: Louisa Potter
Production Manager: Prudence G. Harris
Senior Copy Coordinator: Jill Lai Miller
Production: Celia Beattie
Library: Louise D. Forstall
Computer Composition: Deborah G. Tait (Manager), Monika D.
    Thayer, Janet Barnes Syring, Lillian Daniels

Special Contributors, Text: Margery duMond, Stephen Hart,
    Fran Moshos, Brooke C. Stoddard, Mark Washburn
Design/Illustration: Antonio Alcalá, Caroline Brock, Nicholas
    Fasciano, Stephen Wagner
Research: Jocelyn Lindsay, Eugenia Scharf
Index: Barbara L. Klein

Consultant: Dr. Shing Fung is an astrophysicist working at the
    NASA Goddard Space Flight Center, Greenbelt, Md.

Library of Congress Cataloging-in-Publication Data
Space & planets.
        p.   cm. — (Understanding science & nature)
    Includes index.
    Summary: Questions and answers explore various aspects of
astronomy, including the planets, stars, and space exploration.
    ISBN 0-8094-9650-X — ISBN 0-8094-9651-8 (lib. bdg.)
    1. Astronomy—Miscellanea—Juvenile literature.
    [1. Astronomy—Miscellanea.   2. Questions and answers.]
    I. Time-Life Books.   II. Title: Space and planets.   III. Series.
    QB46.S69   1992
    520—dc20   91-27822
                                                              CIP
                                                               AC

TIME-LIFE for CHILDREN ™

Publisher: Robert H. Smith
Managing Editor: Neil Kagan
Editorial Directors: Jean Burke Crawford, Patricia Daniels,
    Allan Fallow, Karin Kinney, Sara Mark
Editorial Coordinator: Elizabeth Ward
Director of Marketing: Margaret Mooney
Product Manager: Cassandra Ford
Assistant Product Manager: Shelley L. Shimkus
Business Manager: Lisa Peterson
Assistant Business Manager: Patricia Vanderslice
Administrative Assistant: Rebecca C. Christoffersen
Special Contributor: Jacqueline A. Ball

Original English translation by International Editorial Services Inc./
C. E. Berry

First printing. Printed in U.S.A.
Published simultaneously in Canada.
Time Life Inc. is a wholly owned subsidiary of
THE TIME INC. BOOK COMPANY.
TIME-LIFE is a trademark of Time Warner Inc. U.S.A.
For subscription information, call 1-800-621-7026.